BECAUSE
WE LOVE OUR
MARRIAGE

D1602670

BECAUSE WE LOVE OUR MARRIAGE

12 Ways to Safeguard
Your Eternal Relationship

Gary and Joy Lundberg

Covenant Communications, Inc.

Cover image: *Gold Wedding Rings Forming A Heart Shape* © MicroStockHub, courtesy of istockphoto.com

Cover design copyright © 2017 by Covenant Communications, Inc.

Published by Covenant Communications, Inc.
American Fork, Utah

Printed in the United States of America
First Printing: April 2017

23 22 21 20 19 18 17   10 9 8 7 6 5 4 3 2 1

ISBN 978-1-52440-305-8

CONTENTS

ACKNOWLEDGMENTS

THANK YOU TO ALL OUR family, friends, clients, and associates who helped this book become a reality. Your encouragement, stories, ideas, and suggestions were significantly important.

Thank you to FamilyShare.com for publishing "10 ways you are being unfaithful to your spouse and you don't even know it," our article that stimulated this subject in the first place. When the article reached six million views, we knew there was a real interest. We realized we needed to write a book where these article ideas could be fleshed out and explained in depth from an LDS perspective.

Thank you to Covenant Communications for seeing the value of and choosing to publish this book. We have enjoyed working with Covenant in the past and are so pleased to be working with them again. With their guidance, we were able to turn our ideas into a positive approach that clearly shows how Latter-day Saints can safeguard their eternal marriage relationships.

Thank you to Kathy Gordon, Covenant's managing editor, for seeing from the beginning the need for this book. She encouraged us to continue writing, gave valuable input, and in the end became our best-possible blessing as editor of our book. Kathy, you are an angel.

Thank you to Stacey Turner, another superb Covenant editor, for jumping in at the last minute and giving our book the final polishing touches it needed. Stacey, you are a blessing.

Thank you to Phil Reschke for believing in us and what we were trying to accomplish. Your sensitivity and caring touched us deeply. You are the one who gave our book the very title it needed.

Thank you to Kaye Hanson for reading our manuscript and giving us incredibly valuable suggestions and corrections. Her mastery of the written word and understanding of relationships was priceless. She left this earth far too soon. We miss her.

Thank you to Darla Isackson, who helped us with early-on editing. Her input set us on a better path.

Thank you to all who were willing to share their stories with us. Your desire to share filled our book with reality and honesty. Revealing your mistakes and successes so openly proved invaluable.

We are filled with gratitude for inspiring words from Church leaders who gave spiritual depth and validated what we were trying to say.

Most of all, thank you to a loving Heavenly Father and His beloved Son, Jesus Christ, for making it possible to be with our families forever. We hope this book brings us all closer to being able to enjoy that eternal blessing.

INTRODUCTION

"Now is a good time to refocus on what matters most."
—President Dieter F. Uchtdorf

MARRIAGE CAN BE GLORIOUS AND fulfilling to every couple who desires it. This book gives ideas on how to infuse your marriage with continuous fortification and protection, a hallmark of every successful marriage. Specific suggestions and examples of those who have struggled through disappointments and trials, and have yet been successful in safeguarding their marriages, are included. You will also learn from the mistakes of those who fell into serious transgression.

For example, you will meet Jeff, who succumbed to worldly temptations and had several affairs, putting his marriage at risk. You will feel the despair and heartbreak of Maggie as she deals with the tragedy of his betrayal. Discover how the paths they chose changed everything.

You will see how Sue discovered what she needed to do in the workplace to protect and guard her marriage, as a male coworker was attempting to win her affection. You will learn from them as you see what she and her husband, James, did to stop what was happening and what they did to be "on guard" continually.

You will discover some of the clever ploys used by the adversary and what to do about them. The experience of an LDS couple will show how they dealt with the agony of pornography addiction and how they overcame and conquered this enemy of their marriage.

You will also learn of other traps some husbands and wives fell into. Some of these experiences may break your heart, but through the telling of their stories, you will discover what things you need to avoid in order to protect your own marriage. You will also find how strong and resilient many have been in learning from their mistakes and correcting their wrongs. You will discover the joy that safeguarding your marriage brings.

You will find counsel from Church leaders that will prove valuable as couples wrestle with threats to their eternal unions. Since we live in the last days, a time in which the adversary has unleashed his powers on mankind, we need all the help possible to save and protect our families—our marriage.

The words of President Gordon B. Hinckley ring in our ears and tug at our hearts as we contemplate the battle Satan is waging against married couples today. He said, "The family is falling apart all over the world. The old ties that bound together father and mother and children are breaking everywhere. We must face this in our own midst. There are too many broken homes among our own. . . . Can we not do better? Of course we can."[1]

It is usually because of small missteps, almost indiscernible because they seem so harmless and ordinary, that marriages fall apart. We *can* "do better" by paying attention to these small missteps. Couples must be vigilant in a world that so fully accepts and condones actions that lead to infidelity.

Being made aware of these dangers is vital to saving your own marriage and family. Some are not aware of what these dangers are. Because many in the world treat these as acceptable behaviors, they can easily creep into our lives, allowing Satan to quietly and cleverly pull us into his trap. The purpose of this book is to help couples become aware of what behaviors are and what can be done to avoid them. We must be on guard and fortify our own marriages as never before.

President Spencer W. Kimball warned us when he said, "Most of us have vulnerable spots through which disaster can overtake us unless we are properly safeguarded and immunized."

He then counseled us to

> "Put on the whole armour of God," as Paul admonished. With this divine influence and protection, we may be able to discern the adversary's deceptions in whatever appealing words and rationalizations and we may be

"able to withstand the evil day, and having done all, to stand" (Ephesians 6:11, 13).

We must not yield to even the smallest temptations.

Serious sin enters into our lives as we yield first to little temptations. Seldom does one enter into deeper transgression without first yielding to lesser ones, which open the door to the greater.[2]

To help couples become aware of "little temptations" that can ruin their marriage, we have listed some of the key dangers we face in today's world and have given evidence of the damage they can do if not guarded against. Besides identifying these temptations, we also show how husbands and wives can protect themselves against them. In sharing actual cases, we have changed names to protect privacy.

Our work in the field of marriage and family therapy has revealed how serious these indiscretions are and how damaging they can be to a marriage. If couples are warned in advance, they are better equipped to recognize the dangers and make wise decisions that will ensure an enduring marriage. This book is for all married people, regardless of what marriage they may be in. It's also for single women and men who want to be married—those who are divorced or widowed or have not yet married. The counsel we share is for all who desire a happy, fulfilling, protected marriage.

We hope you will seriously consider these safeguards that can fortify and protect your marriage in the perilous times in which we live. We have been forthright—even blunt at times—in the presentation of these safeguards. The time for beating around the bush is past. We feel a little like Elder Jeffrey R. Holland must have felt when he said in a general conference priesthood session, "[W]e speak boldly to you because anything more subtle doesn't seem to work. We speak boldly because Satan is a real being set on destroying you."[3]

President Boyd K. Packer comforts us with this statement: "One thing is very clear: the safest place and the best protection against the moral and spiritual diseases is a stable home and family. This has always been true; it will be true forever. We must keep that foremost in our minds."[4] Safeguarding your marriage is paramount in keeping your family safe in these latter days.

In light of these warnings, please seriously consider what you are about to learn. Your eternal marriage is worth every effort to guard, protect, and fortify it.

Notes

1. Gordon B. Hinckley, "Look to the Future," *Ensign*, Nov. 1997, 69.

2. Spencer W. Kimball, *Teachings of Presidents of the Church: Spencer W. Kimball*, 106, 110.

3. Jeffrey R. Holland, "We Are All Enlisted," *Ensign*, Nov. 2011.

4. Boyd K. Packer, "Do Not Fear," *Ensign*, May 2004.

SAFEGUARD #1

Flirt Only with Your Spouse

"Finding a person to love is the ultimate treasure hunt."
—Elder Lynn G. Robbins

THE SUBJECT OF FLIRTING SEEMS, at the onset, somewhat inconsequential. But your opinion about flirting may change when you read of the dangers that lurk in this seemingly innocent behavior, as evidenced in Keri and Bill's story. First, let's examine what it means to flirt and why it is dangerous to a happy marriage.

You probably did a fair amount of flirting before you were married. That's the perfect time for those playful, appropriate signals that show you're interested. It most likely helped you catch the eye of the one you married. However, note that there is a time to flirt with others and a time not to.

Mariah, a soon-to-be bride, reported that a few days before her wedding she was thinking about her single days. She said, "I'm not going to lie; I really liked flirting with lots of people. I liked the attention." She realized that those days were coming to an end and wondered what would replace them in her new life as a wife. A month after her wedding, Mariah wrote, "But let me just say, marriage is an absolute delight. I recognize that I'm very new to the whole thing and as yet inexperienced, but so far it essentially just feels like an extended afternoon play date with your best friend in the world. The kind that, as it drew to an end and your mom came to get you, would have you saying 'Please? Just a little bit longer?' Only, no one comes to get you. You just get to stay and play."[1]

In order for marriage to be all that it's meant to be, couples need to keep on "staying and playing"—with each other. That's where the attention needs to be. Once those vows and covenants are made, the time for flirting with others is over.

You may think flirting at the office or at social gatherings is harmless and fun. After all, you're only being playful. It doesn't mean anything. You're not trying to get a date out of that person. You're happily married. However, if this is your way of having fun, you need to know you are playing with a lighted stick of dynamite.

President Ezra Taft Benson, the thirteenth President of the Church, counseled:

> If you are married, avoid flirtations of any kind. . . . What may appear to be harmless teasing or simply having a little fun with someone of the opposite sex can easily lead to more serious involvement and eventual infidelity. A good question to ask ourselves is this: Would my spouse be pleased if he or she knew I was doing this? . . . My beloved brothers and sisters, this is what Paul meant when he said: "Abstain from all appearance of evil."[2]

A writer in a national newspaper put it this way: "[I]f you're married or flirting with a married man the sexual tension, while exciting, is still like a fault line running underneath your feet. You don't know when it's going to erupt, but when it does—watch out—because everything will crumble."[3]

DEFINING FLIRTING

What is flirting, anyway? Let's first define what it *isn't*. It isn't the normal fun of bantering back and forth with colleagues of either sex. Good humor in good taste keeps the workplace and other gatherings alive and enjoyable. That's not flirting. Flirting leads you in an entirely different direction.

Now let's define what it *is* so there's no mistaking it. Flirting is looking coyly at that other person. You know—a sideways glance with a little smile that says, "I'm noticing you." A flip of your hair, a slight touch as you pass. It's leaning in a little closer than normal as you look at a report or something he or she is showing you. It's complimenting that person on an outfit with a wink and a smile. It's any action that denotes even the slightest bit of sexual attraction.

No matter what you say about the innocence of it, no innocence is there at all. Realize that this type of behavior is a blatant hint that you want more. It's the gateway to a full-on affair and the possible tragic loss of your marriage. Elder Neil L. Andersen gave counsel to young men that applies to all of us. He said, "Beware of the evil behind the smiling eyes."[4]

SITUATIONS TO AVOID

Here are some possible situations when flirting might occur and how to handle them. In all cases, consider the key person mentioned as married.

- You're Ginny. You've worked hard on a project and your boss is complimenting you on a job well done. The compliment feels good. You can't help noticing how good-looking he is. Temptation overcomes you, and even though you're married, you can't seem to resist a flirtatious smile as you say, "Thank you."

  A flirtatious smile is different than a courteous thank-you smile that offers no romantic innuendos. A smile that says you're pleased without delivering any hidden message is always appropriate. It's the kind you use as you greet friends and family. It's the kind that simply says you're happy to see someone. No batting of the eyelashes or slight lowering of the head in a flirtatious manner. You're simply grateful for a kind word and that's as far as it goes. This kind of response will bode far better for you at work when promotions are offered. Promotions are based on your professional ability, not on your ability to flirt or charm your way up the ladder.

- You're David. You're in the break room enjoying your favorite beverage while reading the sports section in *USA Today*. Before you know it, Marla, a coworker from a nearby cubicle, starts to sit down next to you. She smiles and says, "Is this seat taken?" You pleasantly respond with a polite, "Nope. It's all yours."

"So what are you reading?" she asks.

"Nothing really, just the latest on the playoffs."

Moving closer, she coyly says, "Oh, you like sports, huh?" She's so close you can smell her hair. It smells good. You turn back to your reading. You can bet she's well aware of your wedding ring but hopes that it doesn't matter. You can tell she is in full flirting mode. You have a choice.

The moment you recognize what could happen, you should deflect it on the spot. You check your watch and say, "Oops. Gotta go. Enjoy your break." Then leave, even if your break is cut short. It will give flirty little Marla the message loud and clear that you are not interested in developing a chummy relationship. You now know you need to be on guard and not be drawn into other flirty traps she may set for you. You may have to purposely avoid being where she is. Eventually she'll get the message and move on to her next target.

- You're Cynthia. You notice that Brett has been paying a lot of attention to you lately. He's one of the first to give you a compliment when you do something well. His actions are becoming more than what might be expected of a coworker. You wonder about his ulterior motives. You know he's married. His behavior seems a little too friendly. His complimenting becomes excessive—it's his way of flirting with you. Men know that women like compliments. Hey, who doesn't? Beware when it gets a bit over the top and avoid such situations. He'll soon figure out that your marriage matters to you and that you're not fair game.

  That being said, it doesn't mean you can't enjoy compliments others may give you. It's only when you sense that it's going beyond the norm and leading to something inappropriate that you need to be on guard.

- You're Jared, a counselor in the bishopric. You're having an interview with Ellie. You have served with Ellie for the past year and have enjoyed occasional and appropriate joking back and forth. You're a little uncomfortable as the interview proceeds because she has moved her chair closer to yours and you sense the bantering has gone from innocent to somewhat flirtatious. Though you feel slightly flattered by her flirting, a red flag goes up in your mind. You pay attention and move your chair back a safe distance and go directly into the purpose of the interview. When business is done, you stand, thank her for coming, and open the door for her to leave. You have just sent a clear signal regarding the boundaries of your relationship.

- You're Mandy. As Young Women president, you find yourself in planning or problem-solving situations with Chuck, the Young Men president. You notice that Chuck's usual playfulness has become a little too familiar. He's actually flirting with you. It's flattering but not appropriate, since you're married—and so is he. You realize what might happen if this continues, so you solve the problem by ignoring the flirting and having others present when you discuss youth matters with him in the future.

These five sample scenarios show how easy it is to get caught up in flirtatious moments. They can happen to men or women in most any environment. The results are the same.

Consider the following actual situations that have happened to people we know. We have not used their real names. Discover how flirting started the attraction and how setting boundaries ended it.

Situation 1: James became aware of the closeness his wife, Sue, was developing with a male coworker. He saw little signals that let him know something wasn't quite right. He became aware of it by an uneasy feeling he had when she mentioned the coworker's name. In fact, his name seemed to be coming up quite regularly.

Rather than being accusatory, James told Sue he was worried and that he didn't want anything to harm their marriage. They talked openly about the dangers of flirting and how any romantic innuendoes must be reserved only for each other. Sue began to see the danger of what was happening with her coworker. She did not want to jeopardize her marriage, and she made a plan to set boundaries at work. James pledged that same kind of loyalty to her. They talked about what actions needed to be taken when someone starts "coming on" to you. They made a plan of action that safeguarded their marriage.

Situation 2: Shari worked in a grocery warehouse. One of her coworkers was a man who was younger and somewhat overbearing. He often made blatant but flattering comments about her body. At times he would even pat her behind when she was bending over, and then he would laugh about it. Because she was having a little difficulty in her marriage, she began to enjoy the attention from this fellow employee. As obnoxious as it was, she was flattered to be getting the attention she was not getting from her husband.

She knew it wasn't right, and she gradually awakened to the reality of what was happening along with what it could lead to. She realized she needed to set some boundaries with the worker. In a kind but firm way, Shari said to the man, "Stop it now and don't ever do that again." He thought she was being funny, and he kept up the flirty, far-too-familiar behavior. It took constant repeating of this boundary until finally he got the message and left her alone. In the meantime, she began to concentrate on ways to strengthen her marriage and began giving her husband the attention he needed.

THE ROLE OF MODESTY

Some women dress immodestly to attract attention. That's simply another way of flirting. It's something some women are consciously doing to catch the eye of an admirer. In her book *Sisters, Arise!* author Lynne Perry Christofferson made the point clear: "Suggestive dress and attitudes have no business in the workplace, the restaurant, the mall, the yard, the gym, or any other public setting. Yet we frequently see females of many ages—sometimes even in a religious setting—dressed in a way calculated to draw attention to their bodies."

She goes on to suggest that even though some may be proud and eager to show off their lovely physiques, that temptation must be resisted. She added, "But I've yet to meet the woman, no matter how attractive, who appreciates another female parading sexy dress or attitudes around her husband, fiancé, boyfriend, brothers, nephews, or sons.

"While we're being completely honest here," Christofferson wrote, "let's not forget that no self-respecting husband, fiancé, or boyfriend wants their significant other intentionally turning another man's head."[5]

Women are not the only ones guilty of immodest dress and behavior. Some men, particularly those who have worked out and developed a muscular body, want to show it off in an effort to attract the attention of women. They do this in different ways. Some wear tight shirts, sleeveless muscle shirts, or tight pants, all in an effort to emphasize their toned physiques. Some go without a shirt in places where it is not appropriate. Sometimes they will flex their muscles to show off those biceps in an effort to attract the attention of someone they want to impress.

Flirting also happens casually through body language. It may be the way a person stands, sits, bends over, or any other stance that calls attention to their bodies inappropriately. If your goal is to look sexy by the way you move and place your body, you are in dangerous territory.

Counsel from the First Presidency of the Church in the booklet *For the Strength of Youth* applies to all members of the Church: "Never lower your standards of dress. Do not use a special occasion as an excuse to be immodest. When you dress immodestly, you send a message that is contrary to your identity as a son or daughter of God. You also send the message that you are using your body to get attention and approval." They also suggest, "Ask yourself, 'Would I feel comfortable with my appearance if I were in the Lord's presence?'"[6]

Keri saw the effects of immodest dress in her husband Bill's office. She and Bill had been married in the temple and had four children. He was a doctor and she worked on the books in his office. She watched women—nurses and other office workers—fawn over her husband, openly flirting with her handsome doctor/husband. She said, "They didn't even try to hide it. It was in my face every day. And he was enjoying the attention." She said that some of these women wore low-cut clothing that put their breasts in plain view whenever they leaned over toward him or short skirts that revealed too much leg—and more—when they bent over. She said, "They were flirting with their immodest bodies."

Keri talked to her husband about this, but he laughed it off. He was enjoying the attention. Now here comes the heartbreaking part: he enjoyed it so much he began to have one affair after another with these women. They didn't care that he was married, and obviously neither did he. Nothing Keri said had any effect. After years of trying to hold on to her marriage, the situation became hopeless, and Keri divorced

Bill. This is a man who could have set a dress standard—not to mention a standard of behavior—for his office staff. If you are in a position to do this, do it. If not, do the best you can to protect yourself from the immodest dress and behavior of others.

We must protect our own marriage and the marriages of others by dressing and behaving modestly and appropriately at all times. By doing otherwise we may be giving off messages—wittingly or unwittingly—every bit as inviting as any other type of flirting.

We can't control what co-workers or anyone else wear, but we *can* control what we wear. We can also control our ability to look away and focus on other things that won't stir sexual desires. We owe this to our spiritual self and our eternal mate.

WHAT'S HAPPENING AT HOME MATTERS

If you are having marital problems, you may be more vulnerable to someone who is seeking your romantic attention. An empty heart needs filling. Couples need to make sure that the "filling" takes place only at home between spouses. It may be that a little more flirting needs to happen with the one you promised to love, honor, and be true to. Here are a few ways you can do this.

1. Flirt with your spouse like you did before you were married. A flirtatious smile with a coy look is a fun way to spark things up at home.

2. Sneak up behind your wife and kiss the back of her neck.

3. Touch your sweetheart in tender ways as you pass by him anywhere in the house.

4. Wink at your mate. It's a fun connection. A bishop's wife told us she gives her husband a wink as he sits on the stand. His smile lets her know he saw it.

5. Flirt on your phone. Send each other tender text messages: "Just thinking about you, honey" or "Hi, beautiful!"

6. Slip your shoe off and play footsie with your husband at a restaurant when you're eating out—or even at home.

7. Put an "I love you" sticky note somewhere that may surprise your sweetheart.

8. Wear something alluring, just for your spouse.

9. Snuggle up to your mate while watching TV.

10. Sneak in a kiss at a stop light.

These flirty gestures are equally effective for both husbands and wives. Both will enjoy being flirted with by their spouse. Do it often. Being playful like this will fan the flame that caused you to fall in love with each other in the beginning.

President Spencer W. Kimball wisely stated, "Don't just pray to marry the one you love. *Instead, pray to love the one you marry.*"[7] To that we add that flirting with your spouse may be the very thing that will help make that happen.

LISTEN TO THE STILL, SMALL VOICE

One of the greatest safeguards of all time is the whisperings of the Holy Ghost. That still, small voice will tell you when something is inappropriate. Pay attention to those warnings and you won't go wrong.

Seeking after this divine guidance is an important part of our receiving it. Elder David A. Bednar reminds us, "We cannot compel, coerce, or command the Holy Ghost. Rather, we should invite Him into our lives with the same gentleness and tenderness by which He entreats us."[8]

Couples who pray for the Holy Ghost to guide them in protecting their marriage are on the path to receiving this divine help. Sometimes the prompting will come to one spouse regarding the other. Often what happens when you talk about these kinds of concerns with your spouse is that he or she will discount it with a denial that anything inappropriate is going on.

Regardless of who receives the prompting, we need to heed it. If we do this, we will be able to discern the intentions of others who may be paying inappropriate attention to us or our mate. Following the Spirit will also protect us from giving inappropriate attention to others. Be sensitive to those feelings and turn away from anyone other than your spouse who may be seeking your romantic attention.

President James E. Faust gave a warning that all couples need to heed. He said, "We all have an inner braking system that will stop us before we follow Satan too far down the wrong road. It is the still, small voice within us. But if we allow ourselves to succumb to Satan's tempting, the braking system begins to leak brake fluid and our stopping mechanism becomes weak and ineffective."9

When temptations come—and they will, because we know that Satan's purpose is to destroy families—we can be comforted knowing that God is watching over us. President Gordon B. Hinckley said,

> There is no greater blessing that can come into our lives than the gift of the Holy Ghost—the companionship of the Holy Spirit to guide us, protect us, and bless us, to go, as it were, as a pillar before us and a flame to lead us in paths of righteousness and truth. That guiding power of the third member of the Godhead can be ours if we live worthy of it.10

Follow the promptings of the Holy Spirit in these matters, and your marriage will be protected. You will know what is appropriate and what isn't. You will know when to flee from temptation, as did Joseph of old before the pursuits of the flirtatious Potiphar's wife.

Notes

1. Mariah Proctor, "What I Learned from the First Month of Marriage," *Meridian Magazine*, Oct. 25, 2015, http://ldsmag.com/what-i-learned-from-the-first-month-of-marriage/.

2. Ezra Taft Benson, "The Law of Chastity," (Brigham Young University devotional, Oct. 13, 1987); speeches.byu.edu.

3. Emily Bennington, "Flirting with Danger: The Lesson of Paula Broadwell," *Huffington Post*, Jan. 16, 2013, http://www.huffingtonpost.com/emily-bennington/paula-broadwell_b_2144513.html.

4. Neil L. Andersen, "Beware of the Evil behind the Smiling Eyes," *Ensign*, May 2005.

5. Lynne Perry Christofferson, *Sisters, Arise!* (American Fork, Utah: Covenant Communications, Inc., 2016), 39–40.

6. *For the Strength of Youth*, 6–7, 8.

7. *Marriage and Family Relations Participant's Study Guide* [2000], 18.

8. David A. Bednar, "Receive the Holy Ghost," *Ensign*, Nov. 2010.

9. James E. Faust, "The Forces That Will Save Us," *Ensign*, Jan. 2007.

10. Gordon B. Hinckley, *Teachings of Presidents of the Church: Gordon B. Hinckley* [1997], 259.

SAFEGUARD #2

Spend Time Alone with Your Spouse,
and "None Other"

"To love someone with all your heart means to love with all your emotional feeling and with all your devotion."
—President Ezra Taft Benson

PROTECTING YOUR MARRIAGE BY RESERVING your alone time with your spouse and no one else is an important safeguard. However, we acknowledge here that it may occasionally be necessary to spend time alone with someone of the opposite sex. To be clear, we address these exceptions up front. To further clarify, we are not talking about being the one woman in a group of male colleagues going to lunch or meetings together, or one man in a group of female colleagues. This is not a problem—there is safety in numbers, even if you happen to be outnumbered.

There are situations when one-on-one alone times with the opposite gender occur not in social settings, but rather in professional situations. Here are a few occupations that fall into the category and what to do to protect your marriage in these situations.

- Medical doctors. Though there are times when the doctor needs to be alone to discuss procedures and treatments, a nurse or assistant needs to be present when exams take place. Reputable doctors will be sure this happens. As medical conditions are discussed, this may need to happen privately—always in the doctor's office or exam room. Office settings keep the talk on a professional level, preventing inappropriate conversations or actions. When possible, having the spouse or other loved one of the patient present provides another layer of protection for both patient and doctor. Having someone else present also provides a second witness to the instructions given that may go unnoticed or forgotten by the patient.

- Psychologists and therapists. For clients to talk freely, they need to be alone with their clinician or caseworker. A feeling of safety and privacy as the client shares the necessary information is a must. To ensure that all concerned are protected, sessions need to take place in a professional space. At least one other person should be present outside the closed door, such as a receptionist or family member. With this in place, indiscretions are far less likely to happen.

- Employers and business colleagues. On occasion business colleagues may be required to meet privately in planning meetings or in situations when an employee needs tutoring. Business offices or workplace areas are the proper place for these types of meetings; they should never take place in private settings. Doors can be left open, or others can be present or nearby. When these safeguards are in place, all concerned are protected.

- Teachers and professors. At times, colleagues need to work together to plan strategies to help students reach their potential. When teachers and professors meet with students, subject matter may require being alone with the student. These kinds of meetings need to take place within the educational setting. Doors can be left ajar or open. When closed, the same applies as for other professionals—have someone outside the doors engaged in business or simply waiting for the student.

Sadly, there have been cases when teachers have become sexually intimate with students, resulting in serious psychological harm to the student. Recently such a case was tried in the state of Utah, with the offending teacher confessing guilt. In this case, a female teacher spent time alone with different male students who may have felt complimented by her attention. The teacher's marriage ended in divorce, and the involved students were left with emotional scars. Such behavior is abhorrent and must be avoided at all cost.

In all of the above situations, if a person ever feels threatened or unsafe, he or she needs to walk away. The safest line of defense is to remove yourself from anything that may put you in a compromising position.

Some couples may think their marriage is so solid that there is no way infidelity could happen to them. Husbands and wives are not guaranteed safe travel through their marriage simply by being married in the temple. They must never let their guard down. Satan looks for openings to jump in and destroy that sacred union. What may seem innocent at first can easily develop into a romantic attraction, which can then lead ever so gently into a full-blown case of infidelity and a ruined marriage.

President Ezra Taft Benson gave this clear warning:

> If you are married, avoid being alone with members of the opposite sex whenever possible. Many of the tragedies of immorality begin when a man and woman are alone in the office, or at church, or driving in a car. At first there may be no intent or even thought of sin. But the circumstances provide a fertile seedbed for temptation. . . . It is so much easier to avoid such circumstances from the start so that temptation gets no chance for nourishment.[1]

How Easily It Can Happen

Let's take a look into the lives of a few who were caught in this trap. Carefully consider what happened to ensnare these spouses and ask what each could have done to prevent the tragedy of losing their marriage and family.

Sara and Jared had a great marriage. Both were not only devoted to each other, but to their LDS faith. Their three children meant the world to them. They were the picture of a happy family. Jared was a handsome and successful businessman who provided well for his family. He was on top of the world—he had a beautiful wife who adored him and whom he adored. Life was more than good to them.

Jared's job required some periodic travel out of town; as a result, he had business associates in other cities with whom he communicated regularly. One of these was Darla, a friendly woman who had ideas that stimulated his thinking. Darla lived with her boyfriend, so Jared thought meeting with her and discussing business after hours was okay. What could happen? Nothing, because they were both in love with someone else. As a result, he felt safe meeting with her. Sometimes she would invite him to join her and her boyfriend for dinner. No problem there, he thought. Just pleasant conversation to fill an evening. He called Sara often when he was out of town. He told her about Darla and her boyfriend and said they were pleasant people to be with. Sara thought nothing of it. She loved Jared and trusted him.

One day when Jared was talking with Darla she said, "Jared, it's expensive for you to stay in the hotel. We have an extra bedroom at our house. Come on over and stay with us. It will save you money." Jared, who considered himself to be a frugal businessman, thought it was a good idea. It was a weak excuse, since lodging expenses were covered by his company. The bottom line was that he enjoyed chatting about business and other things with Darla and would have more time for it if he stayed at their home. He told Sara about the invitation and decided to do it. Sara felt a little uneasy about the idea but trusted Jared to know what was best for him.

One evening, when he was staying at Darla's house, her boyfriend went to bed early and left them alone in the living room. They chatted late into the night. Nothing bad happened that night. They went to their separate rooms and went to bed. But what did happen was this: Jared began to feel a romantic attraction for Darla. He realized it had been coming on gradually. The feeling was reciprocated, and Darla did not try to hide it. After all, Jared was a far better "catch" than the boyfriend she had.

Jared felt guilty about having this feeling, so he called his wife and said, "Sara, I'm starting to feel a romantic attraction to Darla." Sara was shocked, but still she trusted Jared. She said, "Oh, please be careful, Jared. I love you." In return, he expressed his love for her.

When Sara shared this story with us, she said, "I regret with all my heart that I didn't take a stronger stand with him. I should have said, 'Don't see her again, Jared. Come home. Our marriage and family are too important to have someone ruin it.'" She said she wished she had reminded him of their marriage vows right then. "I should have taken a stronger stand," she said; "instead, all I said was 'be careful.' How stupid was that!"

As it turns out, Jared fell hook, line, and sinker for Darla. She broke up with her boyfriend and professed her love for Jared. He told his wife, "I'm in love with her, Sara. I can't live without her. I want a divorce." Sara was crushed. What had happened to the trust she had in him? What had happened to their sacred covenants? How could he ruin their family and give up so much for someone else?

Jared divorced Sara and moved in with Darla, professing his undying love for her. It lasted six months before he saw what she really was and left her. Sara felt sorry for him, but said she couldn't trust him, and she wondered what he might do next. He went on to meet and marry someone else a few years later.

Was Sara responsible for Jared's behavior? No. He made the choices. She said, "I'm not beating myself up over it, but just sad I didn't act in a stronger way to protect my marriage." Then she added, "Please warn others to be strong. Don't leave it to trust. Take a stand and fight for your marriage by both of you setting boundaries well in advance. And then continually remind each other of those boundaries and your commitment to your marriage."

Amber, another LDS woman, knew to look beyond the trust and did what needed to be done to protect her marriage to Dave. One day she found a receipt in Dave's pocket when she was taking his suit to the cleaners. It was for lunch for two at a restaurant. When Dave came home, she showed him the receipt and asked, "What's this? Who'd you take to lunch?" He casually said, "Oh, that's the secretary. I decided to treat her to lunch to say thanks for her help."

Amber asked, "Who else was there?"

"Just the two of us," he replied.

Amber looked directly at him and in a kind but firm way said, "That will never happen again. You do understand that, don't you?"

Dave looked at her and said, "Yes. And it won't happen again. I didn't really feel good about it once I was sitting there with her alone. It definitely won't happen again." Dave shared this story with us and said, "I'm so grateful Amber found that receipt. And so grateful she made it perfectly clear to me what she expected of me. We've talked about it since and discussed how important it is that we both protect our marriage and never open the door, even a little, for infidelity to creep in." They have been married many years now and are truly happy together.

Another experience shared with us had a slightly different twist. A pastor was about to invite a woman to lunch to get to know her better and gain a greater understanding of a situation she had shared with him earlier. It seemed innocent enough at the onset, but then the thought came forcefully to his mind, "Don't do it. It could ruin your marriage." He followed the feeling and didn't do it. He said, "Marriage must be safeguarded on every hand. Never open the door to what might lead to a romantic situation." That's a motto every married person needs to adopt.

It's one Harry and his wife had adopted early on in their marriage. When he was living away for a few months as he worked on a post-graduate degree, he attended church regularly. An attractive, single woman in the congregation apparently had her eye on him. One day she said, "I would like to invite you to dinner at my house."

Remembering his commitment to his wife, he said, "Thanks, but no thanks."

She urged him, "C'mon. We could get acquainted and you could have a nice dinner."

He replied, "No. You know I'm married, and it wouldn't be appropriate."

She said, "Hey, we're both adults. Nothing would go wrong."

He said, "No. Thank you for your kindness, but I won't be coming." He told his wife about it, and together they were grateful that they had set boundaries like this to protect their marriage.

SETTING BOUNDARIES

Writer Jill Savage warned, "Don't be naive. Most people who end up in affairs don't set out to have one. Infidelity usually begins with an innocent relationship that, in time, moves to an emotional depth that crosses a line of fidelity."[2]

In his talk tape titled *It Came Out of the Blue . . . Like a Scheduled Airline*, Dr. Carlfred Broderick makes the point that affairs don't just suddenly happen. They are gradual. That's why boundaries need to be set and followed by both marriage partners.

Professionals in the field of marriage and family have found two areas of temptation rising to the top: "the workplace and the Internet. One recent study showed that 73 percent of men and 42 percent of women who have extramarital affairs meet their partners at work." They counsel couples to be "extremely careful with workplace relationships."

They suggested the following boundaries to protect your marriage:

- Don't take lunch or coffee breaks with the same person all the time.
- When you travel with coworkers, meet in public rooms, not in a room with a bed.
- Meet in groups, if possible.
- Don't drink and dance with co-workers at conferences or office parties.
- Avoid cordial kisses and hugs.[3]

A former bishop and successful businessman told us what he did to protect his marriage: "It's important to make a plan—set your personal boundaries—and follow the plan." He was required to travel often with fellow workers, many of them female. His personal policy was to never sit next to a fellow female worker on a plane. When making the reservations, he had his assistant make sure the seats were a good distance apart. He said, "That way you are not drawn into personal conversations."

He also made sure that he and women with whom he worked stayed in different hotels. If that were not possible, he made sure their rooms were in different parts of the hotel. He said, "You cannot be too careful. The distance will give the message you are not interested in a personal relationship." He also said that when business matters needed to be discussed with a coworker, he made sure it was done in a public place in view of others, not in a hotel bedroom. His counsel was to do everything you can to keep conversations with business colleagues on business matters. Do not be tempted into personal conversations. If you have a desire to share the gospel with certain individuals, you and your spouse can invite them to your home to meet the missionaries.

His final comment was, "I don't care what people may think—my marriage comes first and I have worked very hard to make sure it stays that way." Then he added, "The interesting thing is, word has gotten back to me that many female and male employees appreciate and admire the way I protect my marriage, and that they feel safe around me." Then he said, "Most of all, my wife knows she can completely trust me no matter where I am, and I can trust her. We have jointly set these boundaries."

It is important to have a "boundaries conversation" with your spouse long before you are faced with temptation. This is important because, as the Apostle Paul taught, "Sin . . . doth so easily beset us."[18] Sit down in a quiet place and frankly discuss what kinds of temptations can enter into a marriage. Be specific. Talk about items on the list above. Be frank in expressing your concerns regarding what might happen if boundaries are not adhered to. Commit to each other that if you ever feel a need to caution the other you will, and that it will be taken in good stride. Recall your marriage vows and express your love to each other. Take the opportunity when possible to attend a temple wedding or do sealings for the dead. This will help you remember the sacred promises you made at the time of your own sealing. It will keep your marriage relationship fresh and alive.

BE LIKE JOSEPH

Remember Joseph of old who was the trusted and loyal servant of Potiphar? We all know the story of how Potiphar's wife took a liking to Joseph. It's likely she was a beautiful woman, or Potiphar never would have married her. He probably had the pick of the lot, as rulers did in those days. Joseph could have easily been attracted to her, as she was to him.

As a reminder, let's look at what happened:

> And it came to pass after these things, that his master's wife cast her eyes upon Joseph; and she said, Lie with me.
>
> But he refused, and said unto his master's wife, Behold, my master wotteth not what is with me in the house, and he hath committed all that he hath to my hand;
>
> There is none greater in this house than I; neither hath he kept back any thing from me but thee, because thou art his wife: how then can I do this great wickedness, and sin against God?

And it came to pass, as she spake to Joseph day by day, that he hearkened not unto her, to lie by her, or to be with her.

And it came to pass about this time, that Joseph went into the house to do his business; and there was none of the men of the house there within.

And she caught him by his garment, saying, Lie with me: and he left his garment in her hand, and fled, and got him out.[4]

There is so much to be learned in this story of Joseph. What a difficult situation for him to be in. He was at work, doing as his master had assigned. Day after day he ignored Potiphar's wife's invitations to make love with her. Finally, on a day when no one else was in the house—another example of the need to never be alone—when she forcefully tried to get him to lie with her, even grabbing his clothing and begging him, he left the garment and fled from the house. There was no way in this world he would violate the trust of his master, but even more than that, he proved his obedience to God when he said, "How then can I do this great wickedness, and sin against God?"

If ever you are tempted to violate your marriage covenant, remember it is a "great wickedness, and [a] sin against God." It will never be worth it.

It reminds us of the experience of our cousin, whose mother taught her during her dating years to be chaste. She told her if she was ever tempted to have sexual relations with anyone other than her husband, no matter how fun it seemed, *it would never be worth it.* The time came when her boyfriend tried to convince her to sleep with him. As he said the words, she saw the face of her mother appear clearly on the wall above his head and heard her mother's words: "It will never be worth it."

Like Joseph, she refused. She broke up with him and later married a wonderful man in the temple. She has ever been so grateful for the counsel of her mother.

Prophets have counseled us likewise for as long as any of us can remember. President Ezra Taft Benson said,

Marriage itself must be regarded as a sacred covenant before God. A married couple have an obligation not only to each other, but to God. He has promised blessings to those who honor that covenant.

Fidelity to one's marriage vows is absolutely essential for love, trust, and peace. Adultery is unequivocally condemned by the Lord.[5]

The Lord has made this commandment perfectly clear. He said, "Thou shalt not commit adultery; and he that committeth adultery, and repenteth not, shall be cast out."[6]

To emphasize once again, one very important way to safeguard your marriage and steer clear of Satan's traps is to avoid being alone with someone of the opposite sex. Be in control of yourself and never let the adversary, or anyone, lead you down forbidden paths.

Notes

1. Ezra Taft Benson, *Teachings of Presidents of the Church: Ezra Taft Benson* [2014], 223.

2. Jill Savage, "8 Safeguards against Getting Too Close," *Today's Christian Woman*, Sep. 12, 2008, http://www.todayschristianwoman.com/articles/2008/september/22.42.html.

3. "Immunized against Infidelity: 'Affair-proofing' Your Marriage," *Forever Families*, https://foreverfamilies.byu.edu/Pages/marriage/IssuesInMarriage/Immunized-Against-Infidelity-Affair-proofing-Your-Marriage.aspx.

4. Genesis 39:7–12.

5. Ezra Taft Benson, "Salvation—A Family Affair," *Ensign*, Jul. 1992.

6. D&C 42:23–24.

SAFEGUARD #3
Keep Confidences within Your Marriage

"Trust is to human relationships what faith is to gospel living."
—Sister Barbara B. Smith

THIS CHAPTER IS CLOSELY TIED to the previous one, yet presents important counsel beyond just being socially alone with someone other than your mate. It deals specifically with the need to keep the private conversations you have with your spouse confidential. Couples need to trust that each will honor and respect these confidences. These are the things not meant for the ears of others. Satan delights in having you betray your spouse by sharing things that are for your eyes and ears only. If he can get you to betray this trust, he will have his foot in the door.

We will address this issue from two different perspectives—first, sharing confidences with *anyone* other than your spouse; and second, sharing confidences with someone of the *opposite sex*. Both are an important part of being faithful to your spouse, but the second has serious implications regarding the possibility of infidelity.

The confidences that are for your spouse only usually fall into the following categories, though this is not a complete list.

FEARS

Let's say a husband is fearful about his job. He shares a comment a fellow worker said that made him fear he may be fired. This is not something he wants others to know about, and yet he needs to be able to share this concern with someone who cares and will listen. That someone needs to be his wife. Or maybe he feels undervalued at work. This is the same for a wife going through a similar situation. Sharing these worries with your mate is a relief, and it can bring a couple closer when a listening spouse is understanding and not critical—and doesn't run to Mama or someone else with the fear.

Or maybe you fear your spouse is being unfaithful to you. That's a subject that needs to be dealt with head-on with your spouse. Sharing your doubts about your spouse's loyalty to you with others is not a way to solve the problem. If it is not resolved, then the time will come for you to talk with your bishop and/or seek professional counseling.

In the meantime, hold your tongue and keep the confidence, whatever it may be, whether you are the wife or husband. Both experience private fears. Often sharing them with each other makes these fears easier to bear, and you can work out a resolution together.

PERSONAL INFORMATION

This includes any information between the two of you that you want to remain private. One example might be that you are having fertility problems and desperately want to have a baby. Doctors are involved in seeking a solution, part of which will involve trying different methods and procedures—all of them private. Sometimes a couple may even find some of them humorous, but not for others to laugh about. Others may cause tears of sorrow when they fail. This is a private, deeply personal problem. With all your hearts you want to have a baby, and it just isn't happening. As you talk about the cause of the problem, you certainly don't want anyone else in on this very personal part of your lives. That isn't to say you can't tell others that you are exploring possibilities and listen to their suggestions. It's the private part that shouldn't be discussed.

Another example of a private issue might be that your wife has intimacy problems due to sexual abuse that happened to her earlier in her life. She must feel safe in sharing these kinds of personal details with you and feel certain they will go no further. You can encourage her to seek professional or ecclesiastical help, but that will be her job, not yours. You are there as a confidant, not a teller of her innermost secrets. This applies to wives whose husbands may also have been abused.

Same goes for other personal information. Perhaps you are over-coming, or have overcome, an addiction. When the news of your transgression is passed on to others by your spouse, it can be damaging to your recovery. You have to be able to talk about private things and know they will not go beyond your private conversation. Of course, if there is any physical or sexual abuse currently happening, that must be reported to the police or other proper authorities.

DESIRES OF YOUR HEART

If your spouse shares with you a dream or desire that you think seems unattainable, never diminish it by taking it lightly. Listen, and follow the dream with her or him. And above all, don't tell someone else about it. Let your mate do the telling of those personal desires, not you. Couples have to be able to talk freely with each other about opportunities that may seem out of reach or difficult to achieve. Besides, who knows what may happen—"with God all things are possible."[1]

Do not belittle a spouse's hopes by sharing them with others. Some may say to a friend, "My wife (or husband) has this crazy idea that . . ." That is a betrayal of trust. Mocking has no place in marriage.

MONEY MATTERS

If you are experiencing financial problems, no one else needs to know the depth of them. When you and your husband are working yourselves out of a pit, keep it between yourselves. You may always involve a financial advisor, of course, but it's not a subject to chat about at a Relief Society luncheon. General ideas may be talked about, but not private matters. Others can easily misconstrue and make things sound worse when they "feel the need" to share this private information with someone else. That's called gossiping. Don't feed the gossip mill. Keep your financial affairs private.

PLANS

Maybe the two of you are talking about moving out of town or buying a new home in the same town. These are plans in embryo and are not for general discussion. When you are ready to share this information with others, both of you need to agree that it's time. This is the same with any private plans that need to be kept confidential. A few others might include considering having another child, possibly returning to college, or planning to start a new business.

Any of these, and many others, can cause concern when prematurely shared with others. It's a sad day when this happens and your spouse says, "Why did you tell that? We're not even sure yet." A client told of hearing his brother-in-law, with whom he worked, telling another employee private things he had told his wife. It was apparent she had shared this private information with her sister, who told her husband. He was deeply hurt by this betrayal of his wife.

Juicy information has a way of traveling once it hits the ears of someone else. Keep confidences between the two of you and no one else until an agreed-upon time to share with others.

SHARING WITH THE OPPOSITE GENDER
This becomes particularly harmful when confidences and private marital issues are shared with someone of the opposite gender. While the previous chapter dealt mostly with being alone with someone in social situations, this also applies to the sharing of private information with someone of the opposite sex. When you're looking for someone to tell your troubles to, usually in search of help with personal or marital problems, you will likely end up being alone with someone else so you can talk privately.

The desire to share private information with someone can be tempting. It can start innocently, which is what happened to Preston— CEO of his company, married, and an active Latter-day Saint who held an important position of leadership in the Church. Josie was his secretary, also a member of the Church. One day Josie asked to talk with Preston privately in his office. She began to confide in him, telling him about problems in her marriage. He felt sympathetic and listened with the intent of helping her along a difficult path. He had some challenges he was dealing with in his own marriage, and he in turn shared these confidences with her, hoping it would help her realize that she wasn't the only one struggling. After all, as the old adage says, misery loves company.

The confiding continued, and before long, they were sharing more than their problems. It went from a feeling of compassion into a downward spiral of passion. It didn't take long before they "fell in love" and decided they each, at last, had found their soul mate. He took the bait and fell head-first into Satan's trap; so did she. He divorced his wife and married the secretary, who divorced her husband; their actions brought resentment and sorrow to the lives of so many, especially his children. They could not believe their "righteous" father could have done this to their faithful mother. Two families were broken and left grasping for meaning. This true story brought untold heartache into the lives of everyone involved.

Sharing your personal information and problems with someone of the opposite gender, especially in a private setting, can open the door to far more than you bargained for. When you pour out your heart on a sympathetic shoulder, that "trusted" person may feel inclined to give you a hug in an effort to comfort you in your sorrow or frustration. This often leads to more and more time with this same person, where other confidences are shared—confidences that should be reserved for spouses only. Before long the friendly hugs become much more. The tender touching somehow escalates into inappropriate caressing. And, wham! It happens. But it isn't at all what you intended. You just needed a friend to talk to. Warning: that friend must not be of the opposite gender in secluded places. We must heed the counsel of the Lord: "Ye must watch and pray always lest ye enter into temptation; for Satan desireth to have you."[2]

CHURCH ENCOUNTERS

Larry and his wife lived in married student housing a few miles away from the meetinghouse. Their next-door neighbor, Marilyn, was in their ward, and Larry and Marilyn were both in the ward choir. The choir practiced in the evening, and Marilyn asked Larry if she could ride with him each week. That seemed like a kind deed to do for a good neighbor. The problem came in the fact that it was just the two of them.

After a few weeks, she began talking to Larry during their rides home about confidential things she and her husband were going through. This escalated into her sharing things she didn't like in her husband. He was a good, faithful man, but like everyone, he had his shortcomings. One evening as they pulled up to their apartment building, she stayed

in the car and kept talking. It was dark, and Larry began to feel a little
uncomfortable. At that instant he had a distinct impression that said,
"Turn on the interior car lights." He thought the impression was odd,
but it had come so strongly that he immediately obeyed.

This was a protection to them. They were then in full view of
anyone who may be walking by. Light always chases away darkness.
However, Larry realized that the best protection was to not be alone,
preventing Marilyn from sharing any more confidences with him. Her
conversations were becoming too intimate. By following the Spirit, a
potential problem was averted.

The Lord has provided people in our lives to give us help in
times of need, including our home teachers and visiting teachers.
The organization of the Church provides that servants of the Lord go
two-by-two, thus protecting themselves from the temptations of the
adversary. Twos protect those who visit and those who are visited. Twos
provide the members with the added strength that comes from more
than just one caring person. The Lord has also provided bishops and
presidents of quorums and auxiliaries with counselors and assistants
so they, too, are helped and safeguarded in meeting the needs of ward
members.

A stake president told of a time when he was elders quorum
president in his ward. A single sister who needed personal assistance
lived in the ward. He ended up going to her home alone to listen to her
complaints and needs, hoping to give her the listening ear she needed
from a priesthood leader. On a follow-up visit, he told his wife where he
was going and she, realizing the inappropriateness of his going alone,
told him of her concern. He paid attention and realized the danger of
the situation. His wife was protecting their marriage, and he listened.
He didn't abandon this sister; he took precautions by taking another
priesthood leader with him when he visited her.

Several years later, and after counseling many couples as a stake
president, this brother realized even more the need for couples to
safeguard their marriage, including not talking alone to someone of
the opposite sex about private matters. Boundaries must be set and
adhered to.

THE WARNING SIGNS

When driving a car, you will see warning signs from time to time: "Caution: Children at play," "Bump ahead," "Soft shoulder," "Dangerous curve ahead," and so on. Each essentially shouts out a warning to slow down and be careful. The same is true in your relationships with others. Keep your eye out for the signs that are warning you to guard your marriage. Here are a few related to the subject of this chapter.

- Caution: Do not be alone with someone who wants to share personal problems with you.

- Caution: When meeting legitimately with someone (as in a leadership interview), keep the lights on bright and make sure others are nearby.

- Caution: Involve your spouse in every situation possible.

- Caution: Direct people with problems to their bishop. He— not you—is the one with stewardship over them.

- Caution: If you are the bishop, safeguard yourself. Keep a respectable distance between you and those seeking counsel. A warm and tender handshake at the end is sufficient. Hugs may give an unintended message to a lonely person. Follow the Spirit on this, since someone else may perceive your offering as more than ecclesiastical comfort. Though you may need to be alone with someone in your office, be sure that you are not the only ones at the meetinghouse or at home. Always have others nearby who are aware of the meeting.

  If you are the bishop's wife and unintentionally become aware of a member's problem, keep it to yourself. Never share private information with anyone else. It is a bishop's sacred trust to keep members' private information private. If you hear it from someone else and pass it on, that person may mistakenly think you heard it from the bishop. Gossiping about other people's problems is a problem. Of course, if you learn of needs, these can be passed on to the bishop or Relief Society president, but not to others.

A WARNING

The best person in the world to tell your troubles to is your spouse. Christian writer Dennis Rainey said, "Know your boundaries. Put fences around your heart and protect sacred ground, reserved only for your spouse. [My wife] and I are careful to share our deepest feelings, needs, and difficulties only with each other."

He went on to explain that, "Emotional adultery is unfaithfulness of the heart. When two people begin talking of intimate struggles, doubts or feelings, they may be sharing their souls in a way that God intended exclusively for the marriage relationship."[3]

Couples who are best friends with another couple and do everything together can be open to temptations they never considered. Such was the case with Janette and John and their friends Sam and Sara. The wives had been best friends for many years. When they married, their mates joined the friendship. The couples did a lot of things together—went out to dinner, went to movies, and even vacationed together.

The problems started when Sam began confiding in Janette—alone—and started airing his complaints about his wife, Sara. These private conversations continued, unbeknownst to their spouses. Sam and Janette developed an emotional closeness. Sam became a little extra attentive to Janette and complimentary to her. Little by little he started pushing it farther. Janette was complimented by his attention, and it was almost a relief from some of the challenges she and her husband, John, were experiencing at home. It didn't take long before it developed into a full-blown clandestine affair.

Before things had escalated into the affair, John had expressed a concern to Janette about how friendly she and Sam had become. Janette downplayed it, saying there was nothing to worry about.

When everything finally came to light, Sam, who had been the more aggressive one in promoting the illicit relationship, turned on Janette and blamed her for making it happen. She was crushed by his accusations.

Though heartbroken, John did not want a divorce. In an effort to save their marriage, he and Janette went for counseling. The therapist told her the "other man"—Sam—had been nothing more than a predator. Janette admitted she had let her guard down and had been a willing participant. She recognized her part in it and confessed her sorrow for what she had done. She began to realize what a good man her husband was and became fully repentant. Through counseling, they were able to work things out and are happily married.

APPROPRIATE FRIENDSHIPS WITH THE OPPOSITE SEX

According to a group of BYU marriage professionals, contributors to foreverfamilies.byu.edu, friendships with members of the opposite sex are possible and healthy if both parties know their boundaries. As one author puts it, you have to take an honest look at yourself and admit that maybe you can't always "handle it." When you honestly admit what might be a temptation to you, you will know where to draw the line.

These same marriage experts suggest that you:

- Be aware of your areas of vulnerability. Ask yourself: do I promote intimate conversations because I'm curious—easily putting my nose into someone else's personal life? Am I too empathetic and invite others to share personal information with me? No matter how good your intentions, these can lead to too much familiarity.

- Build a solid wall around your marriage. "No marriage is invulnerable. All marriages need protection. You cannot have intimate relationships with opposite sex co-workers or friends and still have a great relationship with your spouse."[4]

"If you're wondering whether you've overstepped any boundaries, Dr. Shirley Glass says three signs indicate that a friendship between people of the opposite sex has crossed the line into infidelity: (1) emotional intimacy, (2) sexual tension, and (3) secrecy. Also, ask yourself, 'Do I say or do things with this person that I wouldn't want my spouse to see or hear?' If so, it's time to take a step back and re-draw your boundaries."[5]

INCLUDE YOUR SPOUSE

Our experience has shown that your friendships with the opposite sex need to include your spouse. If it's an old friend from years gone by where you share what's happening regarding your and their life and the lives of mutual friends, be sure your spouse is included in the conversation or is completely aware of it. Nothing is done in secret. All communication is open to your spouse, above board, and on a limited basis. If communications become too frequent, you can know that's a red flag and time to withdraw from so much contact with the friend. Don't fool yourself into thinking nothing could happen. If you stick with these boundaries, you can be sure nothing inappropriate will happen.

If you've got troubles—and who doesn't?—talk them over with your spouse. Marriage is all about listening and understanding each other. Being there for each other is a crucial safeguard for your marriage. If you don't open up to your mate, he or she has no way of knowing what's hurting or bothering you. If it's the sort of problem you can't talk to your mate about, talk to your bishop. If it's serious, visit a therapist and get the professional help you need.

Turn to God

Most of all, talk to your Heavenly Father. He is always there and loves you no matter what. Remember these words of James: "If any of you lack wisdom, let him ask of God, that giveth to all [men] liberally, and upbraideth not; and it shall be given him."[6] He stands ready to help us with our problems. We need only pray, listen, and press forward with faith that answers will come.

Elder L. Lionel Kendrick of the Seventy comforts us with these words:

> The Lord stands ready to help us through our struggles. We have His assurance and His promise that He will be there to assist us in the days of our difficulty: "Draw near unto me and I will draw near unto you; seek me diligently and ye shall find me; ask, and ye shall receive; knock, and it shall be opened unto you. Whatsoever ye ask the Father in my name it shall be given unto you, that is expedient for you" (D&C 88:63–64).
>
> He stands ready to comfort and counsel us in our season of struggles and suffering. Jacob taught, "Look

unto God with firmness of mind, and pray unto him with exceeding faith, and he will console you in your afflictions" (Jacob 3:1).[7]

HOW TO TALK WITH YOUR SPOUSE

Along with pouring our hearts out to God, we need to do the same with our spouse. What follows is a simple step-by-step guide that may be helpful in starting the process.

1. Pray privately for guidance. Ask for the Holy Ghost to be with you and to guide your thoughts and words.
2. Out of the heat of the moment, tell your spouse you need to talk with him or her in a private setting.
3. Choose a quiet, pleasant place out of the earshot of your children.
4. Choose a time that works for both of you—one that is not quickly sandwiched in between other duties that may take precedence. Allow enough time for conversation.
5. Begin by expressing your love for your spouse and your desire to be able to share the concerns you have for your marriage.
6. Use words like, "I feel sad when . . ." or "I've been thinking about . . ."—words that do not place blame. When someone says, "*You* make me upset when . . . ," it shuts down communications. When you express your own concerns without placing blame on your spouse, it opens up communication.
7. Use open-ended questions. They must not contain the answer; you shouldn't ask questions such as, "Don't you think things would be better if we did (you name what you want done)?" That question contains the answer. Instead, ask, "What do you think we could do about . . . ?" "How will that affect . . . ?" These kinds of questions honor your spouse. It's important for each person's ideas to be equally considered and not discounted.
8. Calmly discuss possible solutions and make a decision. If more time is needed to think about an issue, set a time when you can talk again.
9. Thank your mate for listening to you.

President Russell M. Nelson counseled, "Husbands and wives, learn to listen, and listen to learn from one another."[8]

Learning to listen is a significantly important concept. Knowing when and how to close your mouth and open your ears is vital to a happy marriage relationship. It's the only way a mate has of knowing what's going on inside of you. Then, as President Nelson said, "Listen to learn." Oh, how much we can learn from each other simply by listening. That alone will do much to keep Satan from entering into your marriage. He doesn't want us to show that kind of consideration to each other. It defeats his purpose because he knows we will be more inclined to seek a listening ear elsewhere.

The scriptures give us wise advice on this subject. Proverbs advises, "He that answereth a matter before he heareth it, it is folly and shame unto him."[9]

James says, "Wherefore, my beloved brethren, let every man be swift to hear, slow to speak, slow to wrath."[10]

Proverbs instructs us to "incline thine ear unto wisdom, and apply thine heart to understanding."[11]

These scriptural admonitions are embodied in the principles of validation we have taught for years. Our four rules of validation are: Listen, listen, listen, and understand. The first listen is to listen by giving your full attention—eye contact and all. The second is to listen to the feelings being expressed. Third is to listen to the needs being expressed. And fourth is to understand from the other person's point of view.[12]

When you follow these four rules, you are able to create an atmosphere of caring in your communications with your spouse. This is the shoulder to cry on, to pour your heart out to, to rely on for a listening ear. Your marriage will be strengthened in a way that will make it much harder for Satan to gain a foothold.

A fitting way to conclude this chapter is with the words of Elder Joe J. Christensen, formerly of the Seventy. He counseled: "Make the time to listen to your spouse; even schedule it regularly. Visit with each other and assess how you are doing as a marriage partner."[13]

Notes

1. Matthew 19:26.
2. 3 Nephi 18:18.

3. "Protecting Your Marriage—Marriage Message #38," *Marriage Missions International*, http://marriagemissions.com/protecting-your-marriage-marriage-message-38/.

4. "Immunized Against Infidelity: 'Affair-proofing' Your Marriage," *Forever Families*, https://foreverfamilies.byu.edu/Pages/marriage/IssuesInMarriage/Immunized-Against-Infidelity-Affair-proofing-Your-Marriage.aspx.

5. Ibid.

6. James 1:5–8.

7. L. Lionel Kendrick, "Strength During Struggles," *Ensign*, Oct. 2001.

8. Russell M. Nelson, "Listen to Learn," *Ensign*, May 1991.

9. Proverbs 18:13.

10. James 1:19.

11. Proverbs 2:2.

12. For details, see *I Don't Have to Make Everything All Better*, (Penguin Books, 2000), 38.

13. Joe J. Christensen, "Marriage and the Great Plan of Happiness," *Ensign*, May 1995.

SAFEGUARD #4

Keep Romantic Thoughts on Your Spouse and No One Else

*"Be faithful in your marriage covenants
in thought, word, and deed."*
—President Howard W. Hunter

EVERY ACTION TAKEN IS PRECEDED by a thought. If you want to achieve the goal of an eternal marriage, your thoughts must be aligned with that goal. President David O. McKay said, "Tell me what you think about when you do not have to think, and I will tell you what you are. Latter-day Saints have the responsibility of thinking pure thoughts, of cherishing high ideals. As long as they do, their actions will be in accordance with those ideals."[1]

The key, then, is to keep your thoughts focused on your eternal goals and your eternal companion. The world has no parameters on thoughts. Its philosophy seems to be, think, and do what you want without any thought of consequences. This is dangerous territory because there will always be consequences. Of course, we have the agency to think and do what we choose, but we can't choose the consequences to which impure thoughts lead.

HOW THOUGHTS AFFECT MARRIAGE

Let's say you are noticing how attractive a fellow employee is. Or maybe you have become attracted to your friend's wife or husband, whichever the case may be. Or it may even be someone you serve with in your ward or stake. Is his or her face lingering in your mind? Sudden little thoughts of how you wish you could be with that person in an intimate relationship may pop into your head. The evil one is good at trying to smuggle those ideas into the minds of the faithful. When you let these thoughts linger, it's called "coveting." And there's a scripture about it, too: "[T]hou shalt not covet thy neighbour's wife, nor his manservant, nor his maidservant, . . . nor any thing that is thy neighbour's."[2]

What does it mean to *covet*? According to Merriam-Webster dictionary, *covet* is a verb meaning "to desire what belongs to another, inordinately." It further defines that *inordinately* means to go beyond what is proper.

One of the most tragic examples of this is the biblical story of King David. David looked upon Bathsheba, the wife of another, and wanted her for his own. Her beauty captured him. He would not let the thought of her leave his mind. He had to know who she was. "And David sent and inquired after the woman. And one said, Is this not Bath-sheba, the daughter of Eliam, the wife of Uriah the Hittite? And David sent messengers, and took her; and she came in unto him, and he lay with her, . . . and she returned unto her house. And the woman conceived, and sent and told David, and said, I am with child."[3]

Bathseba knew this could not be her husband's child because he was a soldier and had been away at war too long. King David tried to remedy the problem by having Bathsheba's husband come home for a time, hoping he would lie with her and think the baby was his. But Uriah was an honorable man and would not be with his wife out of loyalty to his fellow soldiers, who could not be with their wives.

No amount of trickery on David's part worked. He was in a terrible mess and put himself in even further spiritual jeopardy by ordering Uriah to be put in death's path on the battlefront, where he was killed. Oh, the web we weave once a step is taken into forbidden paths. If he had not allowed himself to linger and look upon Bathsheba, he never would have committed adultery with her nor had her husband killed in battle.

His sinful acts led to his tragic downfall. The depth of his sorrow for his sins haunted him throughout the remainder of his life. He pleaded with the Lord, "Have mercy upon me, O God. . . . Wash me throughly from mine iniquity, and cleanse me from my sin."[4] Another of his prayers, recorded in Psalms, was, "Create in me a clean heart, O God; and renew a right spirit within me."[5] That is a prayer we all need to offer, but most importantly we should offer it *before* we allow ourselves to be led into sin.

GOD KNOWS YOUR THOUGHTS

We cannot keep our thoughts secret from Heavenly Father. He knows exactly what we're thinking. It was made clear to Oliver Cowdery and to all of us that God "knowest thy thoughts and the intents of thy heart."[6] Ezekiel gave another witness of this power when he told of how the Spirit of the Lord fell upon him and said, "I know the things that come into your mind, every one of them."[7]

If romantic thoughts of someone other than your spouse enter your mind, quickly get rid of them. Make your mind an inviting place for the Spirit to dwell—full of thoughts you would be happy to have God viewing.

In 3 Nephi the Savior gave this warning: "But I say unto you, that whosoever looketh on a woman, to lust after her, hath committed adultery already in his heart."[8] It is never proper to let desires for someone else linger even for one tiny minute in your mind. That means we must be on guard at all times and in all places and in all our thinking.

Elder Jeffrey R. Holland said,

> Love makes us instinctively reach out to God and other people. Lust, on the other hand, is anything but godly and celebrates self-indulgence. Love comes with open hands and open heart; lust comes with only an open appetite.
>
> These are just some of the reasons that prostituting the true meaning of love—either with imagination or another person—is so destructive. It destroys that which is second only to our faith in God—namely, faith in those we love.[9]

THE MANY PLACES INAPPROPRIATE THOUGHTS CREEP IN

The adversary has no qualms about where or when he puts impure thoughts about someone else into your mind. He'll even invade your bedroom. Some so-called marriage experts claim that fantasizing making love with someone else while in the very act with your spouse can enhance your marital relationship. This does not make sense. It's one more of Satan's lies. Think for a minute how you would feel if your spouse were thinking of someone other than you when making love to you. How would you feel if that were the case? It cannot engender feelings of love knowing your spouse is thinking of someone else. Nor can you have tender feelings of love toward your spouse if you are the one having those thoughts about someone else.

These unrighteous thoughts don't suddenly creep in when making love. They find their way into the mind long before that moment. Wherever these lustful thoughts enter your mind—whether you're at work, driving, watching a movie, or doing any other thing—immediately take action to get rid of them. You know how the adversary works. He finds an opening and puts a thought into your head that you didn't invite, then brings it up again and again whenever you allow it.

Elder David A. Bednar said, "Sometimes [bad thoughts] are almost thrust upon us. . . . If you didn't seek it out, if you didn't invite it, it's only a sin if once you've seen it, you let it stay."[10]

You are in control of what you allow your mind to dwell on. If the idea of being romantically with someone other than your spouse enters your head, kick it out immediately. To keep it at bay, you must replace it with other wholesome thoughts.

WAYS TO BE ON GUARD

If romantic thoughts of someone other than your spouse occupy your mind, here are some things you can do.

- Immediately replace that person's image with a mental picture of your spouse. Remember a fun time you two had together. Maybe it was a romantic dinner out. Envision how your husband looked, what he was wearing, and how handsome he looked that night. If you are the husband, remember things about your wife that melted your heart. See her face, her smile, her eyes. When you focus on your mate in this way, there will be no room for thoughts of anyone else.
- Keep a picture of your spouse on your desk at work and at home. Look at it often and think of the tender times you have spent together. Change it around from time to time with

photos of some of your happiest times. Keep those memories alive and fresh in your mind.

- Create romantic memories with your spouse. Keeping love alive takes effort. Plan fun evenings together. Get away for a night now and then. Making fun memories can fill up your mind with the kind of food-for-thought that will nourish your marriage.

- Stay away from that "other" person. If the thought of someone else is tempting you, stay away from that person. If it's someone at work, limit the time you spend with that person or ask for a transfer. Do all you can to protect yourself from any romantic thoughts about this person. "Out of sight, out of mind" may well be the remedy for this kind of temptation.

- If needed, sing a hymn. Elder Boyd K. Packer said, "Choose from among the sacred music of the Church a favorite hymn. . . . Go over it carefully in your mind. Memorize it. Even though you have had no musical training, you can think through a hymn. Now use this hymn as a place for your thoughts to go. Make it your emergency channel. Whenever you find that these shady actors have slipped from the sideline of your thinking onto the stage of your mind, put on this record [of a hymn]. . . . As the music begins and the words form in your mind, the unworthy thoughts will slip shamefully away."[11]

- Put a picture of the Savior nearby and look at it, remembering what He did for you and how much He loves you and wants your family to return to Him.

- Attend the temple regularly. Keep a picture of the temple in your home. Remember sacred covenants made there and vow daily to keep them. Keeping your wedding picture in a visible place will help this happen.

- Pray that your mind will be filled with loving thoughts of your spouse and your family and that you will have the power to resist unclean thoughts. The Savior taught that we "must watch and pray always, lest ye be tempted by the devil, and ye be led away captive by him."[12] Pray for the Holy Ghost to help you fill your mind with righteous thoughts.

AVOID MEDIA THAT PROMOTES IMPURE THOUGHTS

Stay away from situations that foster the idea that having thoughts of someone else is acceptable. Some TV programs, including soap operas and unsavory sitcoms, make fantasizing about someone else seem normal. Some shows fill the screen with bored housewives dwelling on thoughts of having a secret affair. Too many movies show infidelity as a natural way of life. What they rarely show is the real-life sorrow and tragedy such behavior causes.

Though the idea of media influence has been more thoroughly addressed in other chapters, we warn again that these dramatic displays of infidelity are your worst sources of entertainment. Thoughts of being with someone else lead to dissatisfaction in your marriage. Your mind can imagine all kinds of scenarios that are far from reality. A rosy picture of being with someone else is a path strewn with hidden thorns and briars.

We need to be wary of such programs and movies and not spend time watching them. They can weaken resolve to keep your mind free of impure thoughts of someone else. President Thomas S. Monson said, "Many movies and television shows portray behavior which is in direct opposition to the laws of God. Do not subject yourself to the innuendo and outright filth which are so often found there."[13]

With the click of the remote, you can immediately move away from such scenes and find more wholesome entertainment. You can always walk out of a movie. No one says you have to stay just because you bought a ticket. Staying will be far more harmful than losing the cost of a ticket. If you leave early, some theaters will give you a refund in the form of a ticket for another movie. Regardless, leave immediately if the screen fills with immoral images.

Maybe you're thinking, "Well, that pretty much includes most movies nowadays. So what do I do, never go to a movie?" No. Just be careful in your choices. Good, wholesome movies are out there. Read up and educate yourself before plunking down money for the ticket. The Lord expects us to do our homework.

ADMIRING ANOTHER PERSON IS NOT EVIL

Knowing that we must not think romantically about other people doesn't mean married people can't admire another person. It's normal and even healthy to notice and appreciate the gifts, talents, and even the appearance of others. Many people in this world, in our wards, and in our neighborhoods live lives worth emulating. Here's the warning: You will know you have crossed the line when thoughts about that admirable person become romantic, you find yourself comparing your mate to that person, or you wish you had married that person instead.

Some years ago we were well acquainted with a woman who became disenchanted with her husband. He was a good man but was not mindful of her needs. In fact, she felt ignored and unappreciated by him. She said she began to look around at others she admired and wished she had married someone like so-and-so. Then she began to look closer. She discovered that some of these admirable men had faults, too. She said she came to the conclusion to stick with the man she had, and she was reminded of the saying: Better the devil you know than the devil you don't.

Now here's the interesting part. Not long after she came up with this realization, her husband was called to be the bishop of their ward. She was stunned and wondered if the Lord knew what He was doing. Indeed He did. She said that little by little her husband began to pay more attention to her and became more concerned for her welfare. One day he said, "Thank you for being such a wonderful wife and mother. Forgive me for not noticing this before. I'm a lucky man to have you." His experience as a bishop in getting to know the intimate problems of some members revealed to him what a good wife he had. She said, "I'm so glad I stuck with him! He has become a great husband and father."

That's what we all need to do. Stop thinking the grass is greener on the other side of the fence, and stick with the one we married. Give a little time for growth as you work toward building a strong and loving relationship that will last forever. That takes keeping your thoughts focused on your eternal mate and family.

We close this chapter with the words of President Russell M. Nelson: "The noblest yearning of the human heart is for a marriage that can endure beyond death. Fidelity to a temple marriage does that. It allows families to be together forever."14

Notes

1. David O. McKay, "Cleanliness Is Next to Godliness," *Instructor*, Mar. 1965.

2. Exodus 20:17.

3. 2 Samuel 11:3–5.

4. Psalm 51:1–2.

5. Psalms 51:10.

6. D&C 6:16.

7. Ezekiel 11:5.

8. 3 Nephi 12:28.

9. Jeffrey R. Holland, "Place No More for the Enemy of My Soul," *Ensign*, May 2010.

10. "Face to Face with Elder and Sister Bednar," LDS Media Library, video, 23:20, May 2015, https://www.lds.org/media-library/video/2015-05-1000-face-to-face-with-elder-and-sister-bednar?lang=eng#p3s:1301460&p3e:1642900.

11. Boyd K. Packer, *Teach Ye Diligently*, 1975, 46–47.

12. 3 Nephi 18:15.

13. Thomas S. Monson, "Priesthood Power," *Ensign*, May 2011.

14. Russell M. Nelson, "Celestial Marriage," *Ensign*, Nov. 2008.

SAFEGUARD #5

Speak Positively about Your Spouse

"May your marriage be blessed with an
uncompromising loyalty one to another."
—President Gordon B. Hinckley

NOTHING HURTS WORSE THAN FINDING out that your mate has been broadcasting your flaws behind your back. It creates a feeling of not being safe in your own home, in your marriage, or your own world. It also brings into question what being loved and cherished means.

When you are a true friend to someone, you don't say bad things about them to others. Your mate is your best friend and is the last person you would talk about negatively. When you say negative things about your mate, you stop focusing on his or her good qualities. Everyone has a few less-than-desirable traits, and everyone also has positive traits. Obviously your spouse has many admirable qualities or you never would have made it to the altar.

You can choose to say anything about anybody. However, your mate is not just anybody. This is the person you chose to spend your life with—the person you need to trust and the one who needs to trust you, and the person others will see through your words. Your words will be believed by others because you two live together—nobody knows your spouse better than you. You need to make sure the word pictures you paint of your spouse are what you want others to see.

Your words last long and carry consequences that may not be intended. It has been wisely said that you can choose your actions, but you cannot choose the consequences of those actions. Serious and heartbreaking consequences—such as the three that follow—can come from talking negatively about your mate.

CONSEQUENCE #1—DIMINISHED LOVE

Whichever trait you focus on grows. If you see your mate in a negative light, you will notice more and more of his less-than-desirable traits. If you concentrate on his positive qualities, you will notice more and more of those. The consequence—whether you choose a negative view or a positive view of your mate—has two different origins. The first has to do with what you personally choose to focus on. The second has to do with what you may have learned, or inherited, while growing up.

Personal focus has to do with what you normally look for in others and in life. Most people generally look for the good. However, the challenges we experience can change our focus a little bit at a time. When we first get married, our expectations of each other are high. Our love is fresh. Then life happens—children arrive, school is hard, jobs may require long hours with low pay, finances are tight, our bodies are tired as sleep becomes limited—and the annoying traits of each spouse start to become obvious. That's when criticizing each other can so easily become the norm.

Consider as an example the conversation James and Tammy had during a therapy session. "Our marriage and life is in the toilet," said James. "She is no fun anymore and has let herself go to pot, and the house looks lousy."

Hurt and angry, Tammy let loose in response, "You're no prince charming anymore. All you do is come home and yell at the kids and me and tell me how lazy I am. We don't have enough money, yet you go out and have fun with your friends and play sports and don't stay home and help out with the kids."

He quickly retorted, "Why shouldn't I go out? I work hard and deserve some relaxation; besides, you're no fun to be with."

Their conversation—and many similar ones we've heard in therapy sessions—perfectly illustrate how a couple's focus can change.

This isn't limited to younger couples; it shows up in couples that have been married for many years. The symptoms are a little different with older couples, however. Jobs change, companies go out of business, health changes as bodies get older, older children place demands on their parents, elderly parents must be taken care of, investments come up short, and the list goes on. The outcome is the same: disillusionment, criticism, negative talk, and a gloomy outlook on life.

Shelly was good at telling her husband's faults to her parents. They began to think the worst of him, and eventually they encouraged her to leave him. Shelly was surprised because there were many things about her husband that she loved. She just failed to tell that part to her parents. That's when she made the change, stopped reporting the negatives, and focused on his positive traits. Her parents were then able to see their son-in-law in a new light.

Sometimes being negative is learned in our family of origin. In some families, negativity is the normal way of treating each other. Kurt and Jill, a young married couple, came in for therapy. Jill stated she was tired of Kurt's continual downer attitude. "No matter what we do, where we go, or who we are with, Kurt criticizes it all."

Kurt quickly retorted, "Jill is too touchy. I am just being realistic and telling it like it is."

They were then asked about their home life before marriage. They both came from good families with opposite ways of approaching life. Jill told of how her family members enjoyed each other, laughed a lot, and loved to share and encourage each other. Kurt stated that in his family, they had laughed some but it was normal to put each other down and talk negatively about everybody and everything. He said his family was more realistic. Those tendencies persist unless a person is willing to stop being negative and start looking for the positive.

In Fran's family, Fran's mother was the one focusing on the negatives of her daughter's future husband. "Why would you marry him?" Mary Ann asked her daughter as they discussed Fran's upcoming marriage.

"Because I love Jim; he is a good guy and comes from a good family," replied Fran.

"Well, I don't think he will amount to much, and I don't think he'll give you what you want," Mary Ann said as she walked out of the room.

Fran saw the good in Jim and married him anyway. For most of their marriage, Mary Ann criticized every little thing she could find about her son-in-law and kept saying he was not worth much. She was even critical directly to Jim, insulting him and telling him what a failure he was. After a few years of hearing this from her mother, Fran, instead of setting a boundary with her mother, began to believe her and started throwing her own negative darts at her husband. She put Jim down both to his face and to others. The marriage lasted fifteen years and four children before Fran went looking for a "better guy" and eventually became unfaithful. When Mary Ann was asked the reason she was so critical of her son-in-law, she said she was just trying to motivate Jim to be better.

And how did all this make Jim feel? He said he just gave up trying to make Fran happy. It seemed that no matter what he did, neither Fran nor her mother saw anything good in him or his efforts. In our work with couples, we have heard this same statement time and time again from both husbands and wives. Negativity has the automatic consequence of discouragement, discontent, and distancing between spouses.

It doesn't matter why the behavior happens—as a choice or because it was inherited—the automatic consequence is that it governs the way we think and talk about our mate to others. Talking negatively about your spouse can't help but diminish your love for each other. On the other hand, talking positively about your mate will help your marriage and love for each other grow stronger.

CONSEQUENCE #2—DIVORCE

Something happens when a person is "performing" to an audience of friends. Often, normal care and respect gets set aside in the name of having a good time. When the joking mate is confronted by the mate who feels hurt, the retort is often, "You know I don't mean anything by it; I was just having fun." To which the other mate says, "At my expense." And the comeback is often, "Ah, loosen up, it's just fun."

There is a limit. Years ago we lived in a small town in the Midwest. One morning as we were driving, we recognized a car coming the other direction packed tight with a mother, kids, and belongings, pulling a U-Haul trailer—with no father along. We recognized the mother. We did a quick U-turn and flagged down our friend to see where she was going. She told us she was leaving town for good and would not be back. She said she would no longer take being the brunt of her husband's jokes.

As we talked, we learned that her husband made fun of her cooking and housekeeping in front of friends, neighbors, and even strangers. For years she had asked him to stop. He didn't stop; in fact, he didn't take her hurt feelings seriously. She had reached her limit, and she would no longer take his mocking and disloyalty to her. Their marriage ended in divorce.

A spouse can take being made fun of just so long. If your spouse is joking about your faults to his friends in your presence, it can only make you wonder what he or she is saying about you when you are not there. The trust has been violated. This behavior is far from being loyal and faithful to your spouse. Continue doing it, and you may be chasing the taillights of a U-Haul yourself someday.

CONSEQUENCE #3—ANGER AND SADNESS

Throughout marriage, adjustments, conflicts, and hurt feelings can be a concern. All couples are bound to face hard times; it's part of life. During these times, one mate or the other may turn to family or friends to find comfort and solace. This is normal; however, a strange phenomenon often happens. The negative reports are freely shared, but the resolution and return to good times are often left unsaid. As a result, parents and family members are fed mostly negative descriptions upon which they form an opinion of that person.

During therapy, many spouses have complained that their mate doesn't want to go to their family gatherings because they are ignored by family members. The ignored mate tells of overhearing the many complaints and negative descriptions their spouse had given to the in-laws.

We have had parents share with us the anxiety they felt as they were going to visit their married child, not knowing what to expect. After hearing so many negative things from their child about his or her spouse, they were surprised to find a happy couple with normal challenges.

Take a moment and review in your mind how you felt when you discovered someone has been telling negative things about you or someone you care about. It is a helpless feeling that results in both anger and sadness. Such feelings are magnified when it's your spouse who has been doing the telling.

FOUR THINGS YOU CAN DO TO TURN NEGATIVE TALK INTO POSITIVE TALK

Listen to yourself and what you are saying.
Many people don't seem to listen to what they are saying. Often a client in therapy is asked, "Did you hear what you just said?"

The client asks, "What did I say?" Many then admit, "I don't pay too much attention to myself."

Before you say anything, ask yourself, "Would I want my spouse to say that about me?" This sheds a new light on conversations. For instance, Phil told Pat how deeply hurt he was at overhearing what she shared with her brother concerning him. She defensively said she was blowing off steam and didn't mean any harm. Phil very pointedly asked her, "Would you want me to talk about you like that to anyone else?"

She sheepishly said, "Well, uh, no."

His comeback was, "Then why would you say that about me?"

Is there a need to be able to talk some things out with a friend? Of course there is, and this leads to the next point.

Choose carefully with whom you share your problems, remembering the need to keep marital confidences private.
The first thing you need to figure out is what you want to accomplish by sharing. Do you just want to vent your frustrations? Are you trying to make sense of something that happened? Do you want to figure out different options? What is going on with you? This is the time you need to bite your tongue and take a few minutes to carefully evaluate what you are about to say. Resist the temptation to say something you may regret.

Parents are usually the first ones a troubled married person turns to. Children (of any age) know they are loved and cared about by their parents. They believe that most parents want to protect their child and that child's marriage. With this comes an important caution: know what happens in your family when you share. This warning comes from what two people shared with us. One stated if she shared any negative thing or problem in her marriage with her mother, her mother almost immediately called her daughter's husband and told him what he needed to do differently—which only made the matter worse. The other person said any sharing with her mother immediately went to the whole family. Let your parents know that you expect them to keep confidential matters private and to share them with no one else—including family members.

And if you're a parent, please understand that you don't have to make everything all better. Learn how to listen well, validate, and leave the responsibility where it belongs. If you're tempted to share your wisdom, hold your tongue. If you have some helpful ideas, make sure your child understands that they are only suggestions, and that you trust your child to know what to do.

In the article "Marriage Is Not a License to Talk Badly about Your Partner," therapist Mary Jo Rapini said her mother was the greatest support for her and her siblings' marriages. She said her mother had a rule when they got married. She told her children, "You love them, you married them, and now they are family, so if you don't like something they do—tell them, not me."[1] That is pretty good advice for parents. We want to again emphasize the point that if you *do* share your problems with your parents, make sure you share the good things, too.

Don't join in spouse-bashing with friends.
When you are with friends and they are talking negatively about their mates, don't jump in with your two bits' worth. It is easy to get pulled into a complaining session. Often, these sessions start by laughing at the stupidity of spouses. This type of conversation becomes contagious. It almost becomes a contest of who can tell the dumbest thing or quirk about their mate. One might start by saying something like, "My husband's such a jerk"; the conversation rapidly turns into a contest of who can complain the loudest about the jerk they married. It goes downhill from there.

There's a stiff amount of peer pressure to join in such conversations. If you don't join in, someone will ask you to "share" with your friends. Surely you know that whatever is said has a way of being repeated outside of that circle.

If someone urges you to join in this kind of disrespectful talk about your mate, take a stand. Have the courage to say something like, "James isn't perfect, but there's so much about him I love I wouldn't think of saying something bad about him. I certainly wouldn't want him to say bad things about me." If those present make fun of you for taking a stand for your spouse, so what. This is about being a loyal wife or husband—not about trying to fit in with a bunch of so-called friends who obviously talk poorly about the people who care about them. This is about doing all you can to help strengthen your marriage, not weaken it.

It all boils down to the question, "What would I want said about me?" A young man taught us a great universal truth that applies to the solution of this chapter and many others. He said, "I can expect nothing more from someone else than I am willing to give."

Focus on your mate's good qualities.
When you fill your mind with the flaws your mate may have, you crowd out the positive attributes. Whatever is in the forefront of your mind is what will most likely pop out of your mouth first. To counteract this, marriage counselor Terry Baker said, "When you find yourself thinking negatively about your spouse, discipline yourself to remember the good times and the many wonderful traits that attracted you to him or her in the first place. Verbalize these compliments to your spouse often to keep the constructive communication ratio high."[2]

A MIRACLE CAN HAPPEN
The following experience shows what can happen when negative comments are replaced with positive affirmations. A first-time client, Susan, called our office to cancel the appointment she and her husband had for marriage counseling two weeks later. Joy happened to be there and took the call. Susan said, "We won't be coming. We're getting divorced, and there's no way to save this marriage. Just cancel the appointment."

Joy said she would cancel it, then asked, "Do you have children?" Susan replied that they had two. Joy said, "Divorce would be a tragedy for your children. For their sakes, will you do an experiment for the next two weeks? Then if you still want to cancel your appointment, we'll do it."

Reluctantly, Susan said, "What's the experiment?"

Joy explained, "For the next two weeks, say nothing but positive things about and to your husband. Nothing negative. Nothing. Pay attention to every good thing he does and compliment him on it."

Susan said, "I can't think of even one good thing."

"Does he love your kids?"

"Yes. He's a good father."

"That's a big positive. Tell him he's a good daddy. Does he work to provide for your family?"

"Yes, he does."

"That's another big positive. Notice every good thing you can about him. And tell him. Say nothing bad about your husband to him or anyone for two weeks."

"It won't make any difference," she said.

"Will you do it? Will you do it for your children?"

"Okay, I'll do it, but it won't change anything. I can't stand him any longer."

Joy said, "If you still want to cancel the appointment in two weeks, just call. Otherwise, we'll see you then."

Again Susan said, "It won't work, but I'll try it."

Two weeks later the couple showed up for their appointment. They went into the office and the husband started to cry. Through his tears he said, "This has been the happiest two weeks of my life."

The wife said, "It's been the happiest of mine, too. We love each other. We don't want a divorce. Please help us know how to have a happy marriage. That's what we want."

Talking positively about and to your husband or wife can work magic in a marriage, as it did in this one. Everything changed once this happened.

Let your conversations with your spouse and others focus on the good things about the one you vowed to love and honor. That's being faithful. The exception to this rule is abuse. If spousal abuse is happening to you, it needs to be reported to a trusted friend, counselor, and (if serious enough to put you in danger) the police. You must keep yourself safe.

THE PROMISE OF A PROPHET

To keep their marriage strong, couples need to start paying attention to the good qualities in their spouse. President Gordon B. Hinckley said, "If husbands and wives would only give greater emphasis to the virtues that are to be found in one another and less to the faults, there would be fewer broken hearts, fewer tears, fewer divorces, and much more happiness in the homes of our people."[3]

Notes

1. Mary Jo Rapini, "Marriage Is Not a License to Talk Badly about Your Partner," *Chron*, Sep. 14, 2012, http://blog.chron.com/loveandrelationships/2012/09/marriage-is-not-a-license-to-talk-badly-about-your-partner/.

2. Terry Baker, "Don't Let Negativism Ruin Your Marriage," *Ensign*, Mar. 2001.

3. Gordon B. Hinckley, "If I Were You, What Would I Do?" (Brigham Young University devotional, Sep. 20, 1983); speeches.byu.edu.

SAFEGUARD #6
Be a Willing Sexual Partner with Your Spouse

"In the context of lawful marriage, the intimacy
of sexual relations is right and divinely approved."
—President Spencer W. Kimball

AN IMPORTANT PART OF BEING faithful to your spouse is being willing to enjoy the sexually intimate side of your marriage. This does not mean you must bow to every sexual whim your partner may have. Being married does not give either the right to abuse their partner or demand sex. "[Marriage] is a contract based on mutual love, respect and consideration. Each party has a right to their own body, and while consideration for each person's sexual needs is normal, forced sexual acts are not an expression of love, but a purposeful betrayal of the respect and trust which form a solid marriage."[1]

Sexual intimacy is about love, not control. It's about understanding the beauty, and, yes, the necessity for sexual fulfillment in marriage. President Spencer W. Kimball put it this way, "There are many aspects to love in marriage, and sex is an important one. Just as married partners are not for others they are for each other."[2]

Satan knows this. In his effort to destroy your marriage, he will do his best to discourage your sexual affections for each other. He knows if you turn away from this important part of marital intimacy he has a greater chance of turning you toward someone else for that fulfillment. It's one more of his weapons in trying to diminish your love for each other.

Some may ask why having an active sexual relationship throughout your marriage is important. Is there a time when it really doesn't matter anymore? Can't a marriage be strong and happy without it? These are good questions, and the answer is simple. No. Sexual intimacy is important to having a successful, happy marriage until the day you die. It may differ in how it's manifested at different stages of your life, but it never fails to be important. It's somewhat like praying. Having an illness or disability that prevents you from kneeling does not mean you cease to pray. Of course not. It's the same with an intimate marital relationship. If a partner is unable to perform as before, the intimacy does not cease; you simply discover what works for you as a couple.

Here's why:

> Sexual intimacy is a vital part of the marriage relationship because it keeps you connected in a way that nothing else can. When enjoyed by both partners, it becomes a physical renewal of your love for each other—a recommitment of your devotion and your determination to honor your marriage vows. It is a release of stress for both when both find pleasure in it. It bonds a couple, reviving your ability to face the world and all its pressures, together.[3]

Sexual intimacy is often referred to as "making love." With this in mind, let's explore the meaning of the word *love* and how it applies in this situation. The dictionary defines *love* as "a deep and tender feeling of affection." Other descriptions include benevolence, devotion, good will, caring, compassion, and the list goes on. All the good that surrounds the word *love* are embodied in marital love. When these attributes are manifested in the way you treat your spouse, it elevates and enhances the sexual act of "making love."

Dr. Phil McGraw wrote about how a couple can improve their sexual relationship. He said,

> Examine your lifestyle and make sure that you are carving out time to have sex with your partner. Sexuality is a pattern, something that needs to happen on an ongoing basis or else other things will crowd it out. It's about behaving your way to success. Like the

old adage: Use it or lose it. . . . Being sexually satisfied and feeling wanted by your partner is a legitimate and healthy part of a relationship.[4]

WHEN ONE LOSES INTEREST

Georgia and Fred were young and deeply in love when they married. They found great delight in their marital intimacy. As the marriage went on and children entered the picture, things changed for Georgia. She lost all interest in having sex. Oh, she still loved Fred with all her heart, she just wasn't the least bit interested in continuing a sexual relationship. It wasn't that she was interested in anyone else. She was completely devoted to Fred. She just didn't want sex.

Fred, on the other hand, was longing for it. His body ached for it—a normal reaction in most men. To him it was a vital part of their marriage. He was crushed when he heard her say to the couple they were out with one evening, "I hate sex. It's repulsive to me." Can you imagine how that made her husband feel? He was deeply hurt. The very statement felt to him like she didn't care about him. He felt embarrassed and betrayed. He had tried to be gentle and loving all through the marriage, which at that point was about fifteen years.

Georgia was unwilling to go for help with what Fred saw as a big problem. She saw it as a fact—she just didn't want to do it anymore. Because she loved her husband, she did "sacrifice" and give him sex on a few rare occasions. Fred yearned for her to enjoy it and want it. She was stuck in her opinion of it and would not go for counseling.

They have stayed married for many years now, but this missing link in their marriage has brought its own heartache. There is no need for such a heartache. Help is available, but both parties need to want it enough to follow through.

Not all men are like Fred. If sexual intimacy is withheld for long periods of time, less devoted men will seek it elsewhere. And that's crushing to a marriage.

SEX AS A WEAPON

Then there was Ellery. She used sex as a weapon of power. Gilbert had to earn any sexual pleasures she sent his way. For example, she wanted a porch built onto their farmhouse. He was a busy farmer and kept putting it off. She finally played her ace: "You'll get sex when I get the porch." She got the porch, and he got one good night of lovemaking. It was obvious theirs was not a happy marriage. Little did people know the reason why.

Though their names were changed, these two couples are real and these behaviors were their reality. It needn't be that way. Let's explore the reasons for disinterest and discover solutions to the problems.

REASONS FOR WIVES' LACK OF INTEREST

Fortunately, not all women are like Georgia or Ellery, but vary in degrees of interest in intimacy. Here are some situations that may cause a woman to be less interested in sex than she was at the beginning of the marriage. Understanding these reasons can help her fulfill her faithfulness in being an active sexual partner.

- Sometimes she is genuinely too tired. It's difficult to muster interest in making love when she can barely keep her eyelids open. She's had a hard day—running after kids, fixing meals, doing laundry, and, if she's employed out of the home, she's worn out from trying to meet all the demands life has heaped on her. She's just simply done for the day.

  So what's a guy to do when that happens? Preplan, that's what. Pitch in and help with the duties. You know—wash the dishes, fold the laundry, help put the kids to bed—whatever it takes to ease her load. Then the two of you can make it to your bedroom before the plumb-tuckered-out happens. Also, a woman is definitely more sexually attracted to a husband who lends a helping hand and does his part to keep the home running smoothly. These very acts can help get her hormones in gear.

- She finds no satisfaction or fulfillment in having sex. It seems to her a duty to fulfill his pleasures. It's just not enjoyable to her, so she avoids it. There's a fairly easy solution to this, though it takes a bit of doing. First of all, the couple needs to talk about it. He needs to ask her what would make it enjoyable for her. This is difficult for some men because they think they should know this automatically. Questioning his inability to make sex enjoyable for her may feel like a threat to his manhood. He needs to get over that, and be caring enough to ask what she needs.

Here's the catch: she may not know. This is the point at which a couple needs to do a little research and find out what turns a woman on. Even just reading about it together can be sexually stimulating. The wife may feel more comfortable reading about it herself in order to discover her own anatomy and how she can respond to his touch. One woman reported that in an effort to be more responsive to her husband's sexual desires, she started reading *And They Were Not Ashamed* by Laura Brotherson. She said, "By the end of the third chapter, I was so hot to go I could hardly wait to get my husband in bed and apply what I had learned." That's pretty much every husband's dream come true.

Another informative book for Latter-day Saint couples is *Between Husband and Wife* by Douglas E. Brinley and Stephen E. Lamb. Many other books and articles are available to help husbands and wives at any stage of marriage. Search out and find the help you need to enhance your intimate relationship.

When a wife discovers what turns a woman on, she needs to be open to telling her husband what she's learned. Then they can try a few things until they find what works for them. It's all about being willing to find a solution to the problem.

Are there times when a wife will respond to his sexual desires without being in the mood herself? Many times. Here's the good thing about that: if he is gentle in his touching and caressing in ways that allow her to "warm up," she will find herself in the mood before she knows it. Then it can be satisfying and fulfilling for both. Men who rush in with no thought of their wife's foreplay needs will have a less willing wife.

• Sexual intercourse may be uncomfortable, even painful for her. A visit with a gynecologist can usually solve this problem. The solution may be as simple as a need for vaginal lubrication. Doctors suggest that the pain can be resolved if the woman becomes more relaxed, if the amount of foreplay is increased, or if the couple uses a sexual lubricant. There are other causes for painful intercourse, such as vaginismus (involuntary spasms in the vaginal muscles), vaginal infections, pelvic inflammatory disease, or other physical disorders. These can usually be resolved with proper medical treatment. It is well worth taking the time to get a doctor's advice and follow through on a treatment plan.[5]

• She may have suffered trauma, such as sexual abuse or rape, as a child or as an adult. These previous tragedies can put a barrier between a husband and a wife, even though she may want to have a healthy sexual relationship with her husband. The mental damage done by these acts can be so traumatizing that she can't erase them from her mind. In these cases professional help is a must.

The following counsel was given in a booklet titled "After Sexual Assault: A Recovery Guide for Survivors," published online by safehorizon.com:

> If you were sexually assaulted when you were a child or teenager, you may have been feeling the effects for a long time. What happened to you may affect how you view yourself and others, or how you live your life. If you were sexually assaulted as an adult, this may also be true for you. One option to consider is seeing a therapist who can help you sort out how you've been affected, and work with you on ways to cope. In individual therapy, you set the goals and pace in a safe and confidential space. Many survivors find it most helpful to see a therapist who has special training in working with people who have been sexually assaulted.[6]

Your doctor can recommend a therapist for you to see.

Many women with these emotional wounds have been healed. It takes a willingness on her part, patience with how long it may take, and a lot of understanding on the part of her husband. With the right professional help and a loving husband, a fulfilling marital sexual life can be achieved. The words of Audrey Hepburn apply here: "Nothing is impossible. The word itself says, I'm possible!"

- He may be treating her disrespectfully. When a wife is continually demeaned by her husband, called insulting names, being yelled at, and other similar behavior, there is no way she will be in the mood to make love to him. How a man can treat a woman this way and expect her to want to jump in bed with him is beyond comprehension.

If this is happening, a wife needs to set her boundaries. Julie and Carl are a perfect example of this. Carl called Julie insulting names regarding her weight. It hurt her deeply, and she retorted with an equally insulting response. The fight was on. Oddly enough, Carl thought he could still crawl into bed with her and expect her to respond to his sexual advances. She boiled inside and could not—would not—respond.

Julie sought counseling and learned about setting boundaries. She and Carl had three children and she didn't want a divorce, knowing it would be devastating to the children. What happened was amazing to her. It didn't happen quickly. It took time and repeated setting of the boundary before anything changed. She stuck to the plan.

When Carl called her an insulting name, she calmly and firmly said, "Do not call me that name ever again." His first response was, "I'll call you any [blankity-blank] name I want to!" She simply repeated, "Do not call me that name ever again." Then she walked out of the room. When they were in the same room together again, she treated him kindly and respectfully. When he called her the insulting name again, she repeated the boundary, saying, "Do not call me that name ever again." She then walked out of the room.

She held on to her boundary, wondering if it would ever make a difference. Six weeks later she came home from church and found a bouquet of flowers on the countertop with an apology note from him and a promise to work very hard at treating her respectfully. He kept his word and has done so ever since. That was ten years ago. He still treats her with respect, never calling her any insulting names. Consequently, their love life is tender and fulfilling, and their marriage is stronger than it's ever been. A significant side benefit is that Carl is now an active member of the Church, honoring his priesthood.

When a wife loves her husband and wants a happy marriage, she will take the necessary steps to make sexual intimacy fulfilling for herself and for him.

REASONS FOR HUSBANDS' LACK OF INTEREST

It is not only women who may withhold sex. Some women have complained that their husbands don't seem interested in it anymore, even though they are. What causes this? Here are a few reasons to consider.

- Sometimes it isn't as much about being disinterested as it is about a husband being unable to perform the act. Rather than admit he has erectile dysfunction (ED), he avoids sexual contact and appears to be disinterested. A wife can construe this to mean her husband doesn't find her attractive anymore or that he's lost interest in her. That's frightening for a woman. She may even wonder if he's making love with someone else.

   This was the case with Wilma and Gerard. They had been married many years. Their children were grown and gone, which meant she had more time and energy than when the children were at home. She felt rejuvenated sexually. He, on the other hand, seemed disinterested. He avoided situations where they had found intimacy fulfilling in their earlier years. She actually did wonder if there was another woman in his life.

   Finally, she broached the subject and asked him point-blank what was happening. It was then that he confided in her that he had ED, but that he loved her and wished things were like they used to be. Wilma was greatly relieved and understanding of the situation. Together they sought medical help and solved the problem.

   Sometimes ED is caused by overwork and stress and can be corrected by simple exercises to relieve the stress, along with toning down the workload. Sometimes medication may help. There are solutions.

- Men can be too exhausted for sex. Not only do women get too tired for it, so do some men. It's not that they can't perform;

it's that they aren't in the mood and don't want to exert the effort. The solution? Preplan. Take time for sexual intimacy when you're rested. Plan for it and make it a priority in your marriage. It's that important.

- A man may be angry with his wife. If she is too critical of him, always nagging and hammering at him, he will not want to make love to her. If this is happening, he needs to talk with her about it. This needs to happen out of the heat of the moment, at a time when things are calm and the atmosphere is friendly. If it's beyond his ability to do this on his own, the couple most likely needs professional counseling. There's obviously more to the problem than simply not wanting sex.

- He may be fulfilling his sexual needs by viewing pornography. Because porn is addictive, he may need professional help to overcome the habit. If a wife is aware of this habit, she needs to talk frankly with her husband about it without getting angry or insulting. He needs understanding and help. There is more on this in the chapter on pornography. Just be aware that this may be his reason for lack of interest in having sex with his wife.

When the sexual relationship within a marriage becomes a serious problem, do not despair—help is available. According to Jan Shifren, MD, an assistant professor at Harvard Medical School, "Sex therapy is very effective for individuals and couples." In the same WebMD article, we read further, "Sexual dysfunction usually affects both parties in a relationship and should be discussed together or individually with a mental health professional."7

GENTLENESS IS THE KEY

President Howard W. Hunter said, "Tenderness and respect—never selfishness—must be the guiding principles in the intimate relationship between husband and wife. Each partner must be considerate and sensitive to the other's needs and desires. Any domineering, indecent, or uncontrolled behavior in the intimate relationship between husband and wife is condemned by the Lord"8

It is never appropriate for either mate to make sexual demands on a spouse. Acts of intimacy are natural and pleasurable when each is loving and understanding of the other's needs. Are there legitimate times when you may not want to have sex with your partner? Of course. When you are not feeling well, a kindly statement like, "Honey, I love you and wish I could respond right now, but I'm not feeling well enough to meet your needs or mine. How about a rain check, with a guaranteed redemption?"

When these reasons are expressed with kindness and understanding, love will not be diminished. This kind of attitude exhibits a faithfulness in wanting to please your mate. When your mate knows you understand how important this is to him or her—and that it is also important to you—love can't help but grow.

SPICE IT UP

You can spice things up in your marriage by going away for a weekend, just the two of you. Stay in a nice hotel and enjoy the different environment. Just relax and enjoy being together without any of the pressures of home or work. It can do wonders for improving sexual intimacy in your marriage. Marriage needs the element of fun in order to stay fresh and exciting. It's up to you to make that happen, at least some of the time. Otherwise life gets boring and too mundane. It will be well worth the effort.

Blogger Rosann Cunningham wrote, "When my husband and I went on our honeymoon, we crossed paths with an older couple that must have been in their late 60s or 70s. They were holding hands, giggling, and kissing on each other. If we hadn't stopped to talk to them we would have assumed they were newlyweds. Nope. They'd been married for many, many years and were still completely giddy over one another.

"Their advice to us was this: 'Never stop taking showers together.' So there you have it. Be friends, but more importantly be lovers!"9

Keeping sexual intimacy alive and well in your marriage at all stages of your marriage is important. Even though it may change from season to season, caring couples find ways to keep this tender side of their relationship active and fulfilling. As the years go by, it can be manifest in ways as simple as holding hands, hugging, and tenderly caressing each other. These are all evidences of a strong sexual connection that endures the aging process.

An example of this was posted on a friend's Facebook page. Her husband is eighty years old, and she is just a few short years behind him. It was New Year's Eve. She said, "At 11:55, I said to my husband, 'Since we're still up we should ring in the New Year with a big kiss right at 12:00.' He said, 'Great, let's practice for the next five minutes!' (We recommend it:-)" As you can see, many ways present themselves to keep that intimacy flame burning brightly.

The word *faithful* means remaining loyal, constant, and steadfast. Merriam-Webster Dictionary adds an important definition: "Deserving trust—keeping your promises or doing what you are supposed to do." As you apply this to your sexual relationship with your spouse—being loyal to your desire to fulfill each other's needs—you will discover the joy this kind of marital faithfulness can bring. You, too, can have a love that will last throughout your lifetime and forever. It's an important part of how couples of all ages safeguard their marriage and stay faithful to each other. President Boyd K. Packer summed it up when he said, "Mature love enjoys a bliss not even imagined by newlyweds."[10]

Notes

1. "Sexual Abuse, Domestic Violence and Marital Rape," *Hidden Hurt*, http://www.hiddenhurt.co.uk/sexual_abuse.html.

2. Spencer W. Kimball, *The Miracle of Forgiveness*, (Salt Lake City, Utah: Bookcraft, Inc, 1969), 73.

3. "Enjoy Sexual Intimacy—Both of You," *Love That Lasts* (American Fork, Utah: Covenant Communications, Inc.), 90.

4. "Putting Passion Back into Your Relationship," *Dr. Phil*, Jul. 10, 2005, http://www.drphil.com/advice/putting-passion-back-into-your-relationship/.

5. See "Painful Sex in Women," *WebMD*, webmd.com/sexual-conditions/guide/female-pain-during-sex.

6. "After Sexual Assualt: A Recovery Guide for Survivors," *Safe Horizon*, https://www.safehorizon.org/wp-content/uploads/2016/07/Safe-Horizon-Sexual-Assault-Guide-2011.pdf.

7. "Why Women Lose Interest in Sex," *WebMD*, http://www.
    webmd.com/sex-relationships/features/loss-of-sexual-desire-in-
    women?page=3.

8. Howard W. Hunter, "Being a Righteous Husband and Father,"
    Ensign, Nov. 1994.

9. Rosann Cunningham, "7 Secrets to Stay Married to Your Spouse
    Well into the Golden Years," blog, http://rosanncunningham.
    com/secrets-stay-married-spouse-golden-years/.

10. *Eternal Marriage Student Manual*, "Intimacy in Marriage," 2003,
    https://www.lds.org/manual/eternal-marriage-student-manual/
    intimacy-in-marriage?lang=eng.

SAFEGUARD #7
Be More Devoted to Your Spouse Than to the Internet

"Sometimes the most productive 'point and click' application is that of pointing our finger at the power button and clicking our digital devices off."
—Elder Scott. D. Whiting

IN SPITE OF ITS AMAZING ability to help us in appropriate ways, the Internet is fast becoming a common intruder into the lives of married people. Its allure takes over the lives of far too many spouses, pushing their wives or husbands out of any meaningful marital relationship. We can learn from Elder Russell M. Nelson's observations:

> On a recent flight, I sat behind a husband and wife. She obviously loved her husband. As she stroked the back of his neck I could see her wedding ring. She would nestle close to him and rest her head upon his shoulder, seeking his companionship.
>
> In contrast, he seemed totally oblivious to her presence. He was focused solely upon an electronic game player. During the entire flight, his attention was riveted upon that device. Not once did he look at her, speak to her, or acknowledge her yearning for affection.
>
> His inattention made me feel like shouting: "Open your eyes, man! Can't you see? Pay attention! Your wife loves you! She needs you!"[1]

It's sad neglect when husbands or wives let electronic devices take precedence over their spouses. Far too often a consuming Internet focus in one spouse's life has led to divorce. This type of unfaithfulness comes in many forms. We'll discuss four of the major cyberspace temptations couples need to guard against. Others exist, but these seem to rise to the top.

1. Emailing and Texting

Emailing and texting are valuable ways to communicate with people with whom you interact in normal, everyday life. At work and in Church callings these are the two most common ways to get the word out to those with whom you work. We're not suggesting you give up these means of communication. What we *are* suggesting is that you be careful about becoming too personal in those communications. If the element of familiarity enters in, back off. Keep communications appropriate for the office—the kind of communication that could be read by your supervisor or coworkers without you being embarrassed.

How easily can familiarity slip in? Just a simple comment like "Are you married?" can be the beginning. That comment has nothing to do with business. Say that, and you've crossed the line. If a business associate says that to you, he or she has crossed the line. It implies that you or the other person is looking for a more personal relationship, even if that's not what was intended.

Be cautious in your communications and avoid sharing *any* of your personal information. Whenever you get personal, you know you've gone too far. Keep your emails and texts at work about business, and you'll be protecting your marriage. Never say anything in an email or text to someone of the opposite sex that you would not want your spouse to read. Once a relationship has crossed the line, some people have gone so far as to open a separate secret email address so no one else can read the correspondence. If you find yourself in this position, we strongly urge you to immediately cancel that email address and cease communication with that person. Whatever it takes, protect your marriage.

The same boundary applies to texting. Also important is the need to guard your personal time with your spouse by limiting texting with others, regardless of who it may be, when you are together. We have witnessed couples out to dinner with one or the other texting as the spouse sits there being ignored. Or they're both texting others while ignoring each other. That's not only disrespectful, but it says your spouse doesn't really matter enough to receive your full attention while on a date. Date nights are meant to bring you closer together, not for communicating with business associates or friends. Give each other your undivided attention in conversations, including eye-to-eye contact and smiles. That's what being a faithful spouse is all about.

2. CHAT ROOMS

Having a conversation on the Internet with someone other than your spouse may seem innocent at first. Maybe you're bored and just looking for something interesting to do. The Internet is loaded with chat room invitations for lonely or curious adults. However tempting it may be, married individuals should never indulge in this activity.

Finding something interesting to do in the depths of the unknown may be intriguing, but you will be treading on treacherously thin ice. If communication continues and conversations take on a more intimate flavor, this becomes a betrayal of trust. It's like teenagers sneaking into a closet to make out where no one can see them. Married people becoming involved in an Internet chat room, just for the fun of it, can be a serious threat to their marriage.

Beatriz Mileham of the University of Gainesville in Florida did a study on the effect of Internet chat rooms on marriages. She wrote: "The Internet will soon become the most common form of infidelity, if it isn't already."

Further analysis of her study shows that "with 649 million Internet users worldwide, chat rooms were a fatal attraction for many married people seeking sexual thrills and romantic adventure.

"In the vast majority of cases, spouses who had Internet encounters with the opposite sex did not think they were doing anything wrong." The study also revealed that "on-line adultery caused the same feelings of hurt, anger and betrayal as skin-to-skin contact.

"And in many cases what started out as innocent fun ended up as a full-blown affair."[2]

Apparently, what seemed like innocent Internet chatting went quickly into dangerous territory. "The research found an escalating quality to these on-line contacts. Many participants reported that innocent, friendly exchanges progressed quickly to strong desires for sexual relationships.

"Almost a third of the study participants went on to meet the person with whom they had made contact.

"Of these, all but two ended up having a real-life affair."[3]

You can only imagine how devastating this would be to a marriage. Lyle could tell you how tragic it was for him. His wife, Connie, started looking for companionship on the Internet because Lyle was gone long hours for his job. He was devoted to his wife and three children, working hard to provide a living for them. She thought it might be fun to find a male friend to chat with on the Internet to fill her lonely hours.

Big mistake.

What starts out innocent and seems like a simple friendship can quickly change to titillating conversation that release hormones much like those experienced by pornography addicts. A person can experience a chemical high, and too often the recipient wants more, and on goes the conversation—deeper and deeper. What is mistaken for a growing love is no more than online sexual infatuation.

That's what was happening to Connie. One day she announced to her husband that she had found her true love on the Internet and wanted a divorce. He could hardly believe what he was hearing. How could she do this to him and to their family? He could not convince her otherwise. She took their children and left to be with this newfound love—a tragedy not only for him but for their children, who were now separated from their father, who loved them. In the end, the relationship with her "true love" turned out to be nothing more than an affair that ended almost before it began. This online lover was far from wanting a lasting relationship. Connie ended up moving in with her parents rather than apologize to her husband and try to mend her marriage. It was a very sad result from what started out to be someone looking for a little companionship in the wrong place.

This scenario doesn't happen only to women. On his website marriagebuilders.com, Willard F. Harley, PhD, receives letters from readers often asking for help with their marital problems. One such letter was from a husband, married two years, telling of his own online romance that he describes as becoming "highly emotional, rewarding and sexual. . . ." He felt compelled to meet this woman, even though he said, "I know it could destroy my marriage. . . . I love my wife and would never want to do anything to hurt her." If that were true, he would immediately stop this online relationship because there is no question—it will hurt her.

Dr. Harley did not beat around the bush. He boldly replied,

> You're right when you say, "it could destroy my marriage." E-mail romances are common and have ruined many marriages. As with most affairs, once the relationship gets real, it falls apart. . . .
>
> Affairs are addictions, both in real life and on the Internet. But the bottom line is that you must completely sever your relationship with this woman, as difficult as it will be for you to do. Even though you feel compelled to meet her, don't let the relationship go any farther than it already has. . . .
>
> You are certainly on the right track to recognize your Internet relationship as a compulsion. It is a compulsion, and the sooner you can get out of it, the better. Then, learn to add to your marriage what it is that you are missing. It will help prevent you from getting into a mess like this in the future.[4]

3. FACEBOOK

Facebook is a highly popular social media site. It's everywhere. According to the *Washington Post*, in a recent announcement from the founders of the site, "its monthly active users cleared 1.35 billion— roughly equal the population of China, and 9 percent larger than that of India."[5] This is a huge network.

Facebook has its good points. It's a quick and fun way to stay connected to family and friends. Seeing a picture and report of a grandchild performing or doing something fun with the family is an instant reward. Keeping up on the progress of a friend or loved one who is undergoing medical treatment is also a blessing. Many good things happen on Facebook.

The problem is that, unless controlled, Facebook can become your enemy. It can steal away precious time that could be better spent with your spouse and family. In some cases it's a relationship thief that creates marital conflict, ever so slowly developing into an online affair. "[Some] marriage counselors are sending a warning to even happily married couples: Facebook affairs are threatening healthy couples, too."[6]

Because of the increase in divorce caused by Facebook relationships, one writer stated, "Maybe they should change the marriage vows to include, 'until Facebook do us part. . . . The social networking site can essentially pour kerosene on 'old flames.'"[7]

A survey of 205 Facebook users conducted by doctoral student Russell Clayton found that of "Facebook users between the ages of 18 and 82, 79 percent . . . reported being in a romantic relationship." They were asked if their use of social media had instigated conflict with their current or former partners.

Clayton's findings showed that there *was* a definite connection. "Previous research has shown that the more a person in a romantic relationship uses Facebook, the more likely they are to monitor their partner's Facebook activity more stringently, which can lead to feelings of jealousy," Clayton said. "Facebook-induced jealousy may lead to arguments concerning past partners. Also, our study found that excessive Facebook users are more likely to connect or reconnect with other Facebook users, including previous partners, which may lead to emotional and physical cheating . . . ." Clayton recommends "limiting Facebook usage in order to achieve a healthy, lasting relationship."[8]

Can there be healthy friendships on Facebook? In some cases the answer is yes, but with boundaries set by husbands and wives. One of our own Facebook friends said, "My own parents refuse to open up a Facebook account, because they've 'heard' of divorces caused by it. They miss out on a lot of news with our grandchildren, so I chide them that even our Church leaders have Facebook accounts. When this and similar forums are brought up, I always remind people that it's not Facebook, or necessarily chat rooms, or work environment to blame. It's almost like gun or weapon control. The weapons don't kill, people do."

Our friend made a good point when he went on to say, "Facebook doesn't cause extramarital infidelity, people do. Adultery can happen at a public library, workplace, or any other public venue. True, 'meeting places' can facilitate faux pas, but they are not the cause. I have female acquaintances that *we* (my wife and I) connected with from my high school days and those relationships have always been appropriate. I think the key is that married people pursue relationships together—no secrets. Facebook has been an enriching part of our lives, through friendships with friends and loved ones. There is a wealth of information that is useful within proper boundaries. Defining those boundaries at the outset is key."

This friend brings out a couple of key factors that are imperative in avoiding a Facebook affair.

1. He and his wife shared the friendships together—no secrets. He said, "If there is a woman I am friends with, *we* (my wife and I) are friends with her. If there is a man my wife is friends with, *we* (my wife and I) are friends with him. It all starts with environment, physical and virtual. Secrets outside the marriage where one spouse finds comfort/consolation with an opposite gender 'friend' carries risk. It's when people deem those 'innocent,' seemingly harmless modes of 'pairing off' styles of relationships as harmless—even online—that there is potential for devastation down the road."

2. Limit the time spent on Facebook. This allows for more time to spend together in pursuits that enrich a couple's relationship, as well as relationships with their family.

Our point is: be careful. Do not engage in conversations on Facebook that have any possibility of leading to improper relationships.

4. ONLINE GAMING

Playing online games can snatch a person out of reality into a fascinating world of fantasy. When this fascination consumes a spouse, it can clearly affect the marriage relationship. What defines a gaming addiction? According to an article by Jerald J. Block, MD, in *The American Journal of Psychiatry*, Internet addiction (which includes gaming) consists of these four components: "1) excessive use, often associated with a loss of sense of time or a neglect of basic drives; 2) withdrawal, including feelings of anger, tension, and/or depression when the computer is inaccessible; 3) . . . the need for better computer equipment, more software, or more hours of use; and 4) negative repercussions, including arguments, lying, poor achievement, social isolations, and fatigue."9

These four components became evident in a comment posted on the On-Line Gamers Anonymous site. A husband told how he and his wife had been involved in online gaming together until it started to take over their lives. Seeing how it was replacing any intimacy they had together, he withdrew. She, on the other hand, was too hooked. He said, "She used to smile when she talked to me when I sat next to her at my computer. Now she'll have that blank look on her face, or say a rehearsed 'I love you, too' when I tell her I love her, with no smile or even any emotion. But, God forbid, someone in the game sends her a message, suddenly her face lights up and a smile comes across her face as she replies to one of her in-game friends. Yeah, that makes me feel just wonderful; it happens all the time now. So now, I just don't speak."

He went on, lamenting, "I feel like the alone time I had with my wife when I came home from work is now something I have to share with twenty-five other people on a voice chat server. I have to let those people in my house every night and listen to them talk. I didn't mind it at first, but when my wife converses with them more than me, then it's a problem."

He came to the conclusion that he needed to "separate from the game and just start focusing on the house more and make sure my kids aren't too scarred by my wife constantly being on this game." He ended his story with, "I'm hurt, sad, and broken. But the only course of action I can take is to leave the game and let her figure it out on her own. I'll be here if she wants me, but I'm not going to wait forever."

This is not a lone cry in the wilderness. It's all too common. We've heard many wives weep over the way their husbands are addicted to their online or other video games. They feel alone and ignored by the very one with whom they should be sharing life.

Elder David A. Bednar raised a warning voice when he said, "We should not squander and damage authentic relationships by obsessing over contrived ones. 'Nearly 40% of men and 53% of women who play online games said their virtual friends were equal to or better than their real-life friends, according to a survey of 30,000 gamers conducted by . . . a recent Ph.D. graduate from Stanford University. More than a quarter of gamers [who responded indicated that] the emotional highlight of the past week occurred in a computer world.'"10

Our warning is to be extra careful when becoming involved in online gaming. Limit your time and don't ignore your spouse and family. Replacing them with unknown players is simply exchanging gold for garbage. Don't let gaming interfere with your marriage and family life.

WHATEVER THE VENUE

Whatever method you use to engage romantically online with someone other than your spouse, the results are almost always the same. A writer for the *Washington Post* said, "Affairs often feel like love." Then, quoting a woman who had an online affair, continued, "You get very close emotionally and physically very quickly, but it's a fake closeness. For him, it was out of sight, out of mind. For me, the day after was always the hardest."

"The relationship can never go anywhere. You're making a banquet out of crumbs." She discounted the possibility that the affair would lead to marriage. "Even if a person gets divorced, the new relationship is still based on a lie," she said.11

Marriage experts on foreverfamilies.com said, "Remember that infidelity doesn't always include sex. Emotional infidelity can breach marital trust and become as debilitating to your marriage as physical adultery. If you are sharing intimate emotional closeness with someone of the opposite sex other than your spouse in any arena . . . *stop!*"12

The bottom line is this: whatever the affair may look like, it's still an affair. It will never be worth it. Heartache and sorrow can't help but be the result.

A VOICE OF WARNING

Elder Bednar continued with this admonition:

> I raise an apostolic voice of warning about the potentially stifling, suffocating, suppressing, and constraining impact of some kinds of cyberspace interactions and experiences upon our souls. The concerns I raise are not new; they apply equally to other types of

media, such as television, movies, and music. But in a
cyber world, these challenges are more pervasive and
intense. I plead with you to beware of the sense-dulling
and spiritually destructive influence of cyberspace tech-
nologies that are used to produce high fidelity and that
promote degrading and evil purposes.[13]

We must be continually on guard and do all we can to protect
our marriage and family. Multitudes of other online distractions can
interfere with a marriage and family responsibilities. Pinterest, for
example, can provide many good ideas for families, but when done in
excess it can steal away precious time for the very ones whose lives you
are trying to enhance through your Pinterest searching. The same goes
for other social media sites. Be careful. Be wise.

FIND THE GOOD ONLINE

Use the Internet to bless your marriage. Read articles and talks that
will give you ideas for improving your marriage relationship. Besides
the inspiring talks by our General Authorities, many helpful sites are
available, such as foreverfamilies.byu.edu, a site sponsored by the School
of Family Life at Brigham Young University. Smartmarriage.com is
another good site filled with helpful suggestions to strengthen marriages.
Best of all, go to LDS.org and find the scriptures at your fingertips, as
well as *Ensign* articles and many other helps for creating an eternal
family. Make sure the reading of these is not done in excess, at the
exclusion of being with and interacting with your spouse. Together you
can share the ideas you glean from these worthy sources.

Along with this, when you're in a romantic mood, send that kind
of message to your sweetheart. A loving, flirtatious email or text from
a spouse shot across cyberspace can reignite marital romance. Spend
your creative juices on messages and actions that show your spouse you
love him or her.

In the end, the most effective way to safeguard your marriage is to
keep it alive and fulfilling. Spend your time and energy finding ways to
please your spouse. Have fun together. Share meaningful conversations
together. Enjoy and help your children together. Pray together. Be
together.

Notes

1. Russell M. Nelson, "Nurturing Marriage," *Ensign*, May 2006.

2. "Internet cheats cause divorce," *Daily Mail*, http://www.dailymail.co.uk/femail/article-189203/Internet-cheats-cause-divorce.html.

3. Ibid.

4. "Infidelity on the Internet," *Marriage Builders*, http://www.marriagebuilders.com/graphic/mbi5028b_qa.html.

5. Caitlin Dewey, "Almost as Many People Use Facebook as Live in the Entire Country of China," *The Washington Post*, Oct. 29, 2014, http://www.washingtonpost.com/news/the-intersect/wp/2014/10/29/almost-as-many-people-use-facebook-as-live-in-the-entire-country-of-china/.

6. Therese Borchard, "Does the Internet Promote or Damage Marriage?" *Huffington Post*, Apr. 5, 2011, http://www.huffingtonpost.com/therese-borchard/does-the-Internet-promote_b_841401.html.

7. Ibid.

8. "Facebook, Divorce Linked in New Study," *Huffington Post*, Jun. 10, 2013, http://www.huffingtonpost.com/2013/06/06/facebook-divorce-linked-i_n_3399727.html.

9. Jerald J. Block, "Issues for DSM-V: Internet Addiction," *American Journal of Psychology* 165, no. 3 (Mar. 2008): 306, http://ajp.psychiatryonline.org/doi/pdfplus/10.1176/appi.ajp.2007.07101556.

10. David A. Bednar, "Things as They Really Are," *Ensign*, Jun. 2010.

11. Pam Gerhardt, "The Emotional Cost of Infidelity," *The Washington Post*, Mar. 30, 1999, http://www.washingtonpost.com/wp-srv/national/health/march99/infid033099.htm.

12. "Immunized Against Infidelity: 'Affair-proofing' Your Marriage," *Forever Families*, https://foreverfamilies.byu.edu/Pages/marriage/IssuesInMarriage/Immunized-Against-Infidelity-Affair-proofing-Your-Marriage.aspx; emphasis added.

13. David A. Bednar, "Things as They Really Are," *Ensign*, Jun. 2010.

SAFEGUARD #8
Stay Away from Pornography

"[Pornography] is one of the most damning influences on earth."
—Elder Richard G. Scott

THERE IS NO SOFT-PEDALING THE destruction pornography causes in a marriage. President Gordon B. Hinckley said, "[Pornography] is like a raging storm, destroying individuals and families, utterly ruining what was once wholesome and beautiful."[1]

Our desire in writing this chapter is to stop this "raging storm" from ruining your marriage and family. When talking about pornography and marriage, we first want to share some preventive measures, and then explore recovery for those who have fallen victim to this Satanic snare.

REMEMBER THE SANCTITY AND COMMITMENT OF MARRIAGE

After Adam was created, the Lord said, "It is not good that man should be alone; I will make him an help meet."[2] When Eve was introduced to Adam, he recognized her importance in that she was "bone of my bones, and flesh of my flesh."[3] The next verse introduces the concept of marriage and the commitment it brings: "Therefore shall a man leave his father and mother, and shall cleave unto his wife: and they shall be one flesh."[4] In this short verse, we learn that husband and wife set up their own home, the spouse becomes the priority over one's family of origin, they hold fast to each other with unwavering loyalty, they become one in purpose, and they multiply and replenish the earth.

As President Spencer W. Kimball states, "Marriage presupposes total allegiance and total fidelity. Each spouse takes the partner with the understanding that he or she gives totally to the spouse all the heart, strength, loyalty, honor, and affection, with all dignity."[5]

To add emphasis to President Kimball's statement, we read, "Thou shalt love thy wife with all thy heart, and shalt cleave unto her and none else."[6] The words "all thy heart" and "none else" leave no wiggle room.

A few short scriptures add direction in our marriages and each applies to both husband and wife:

- "Rejoice with the wife of thy youth . . . and be thou ravished always with her love."[7]
- "Live joyfully with the wife whom thou lovest."[8]
- "Let the husband render unto the wife due benevolence: and likewise also the wife unto the husband."[9]
- "The wife hath not power of her own body, but the husband: and likewise also the husband hath not power of his own body, but the wife."[10]
- "Husbands, love your wives, even as Christ also loved the church, and gave himself for it. . . ."[11]

President Gordon B. Hinckley adds, "Brethren, treat your wives with love and respect and kindness. And, wives, you treat your husbands with love and respect and kindness."[12]

The prophets in our dispensation have encouraged us all to marry in the temple. Our union is done with the goal to build a marriage that will last for eternity. This goal gives greater meaning to our commitment to each other and to our family, and it underscores the need to be ever vigilant in protecting our sacred covenants. We have to review constantly what is needed and expected to keep us alert.

THE GREAT DESTROYER

Elder Boyd K. Packer stated, "The single purpose of Lucifer is to oppose the great plan of happiness, to corrupt the purest, most beautiful and appealing experiences of life: romance, love, marriage, and parenthood."[13] One of his most effective weapons is pornography.

Pornography fights against marriage in an individual way. It starts small and grows quickly, destroying from the inside out. It substitutes the unreal for the real. It creates a chemical reaction in the brain that is hard to fight and get rid of because it often takes over all ability to reason.

Authors Mark Chamberlain and Geoff Steurer describe this process: "One of the reasons pornography draws people in and keeps them hooked is that it offers physical and emotional soothing in a way that doesn't require as much emotional risk as reaching out to a partner would." They further state, "Pornography can mimic the experience of being comforted by a loving attachment figure in that it activates some of the same physiological soothing mechanisms. Plus, it's always available, easy to access, doesn't require us to be vulnerable, and consistently delivers the desired relief." They also give the down side: "The relief too quickly gives way to feelings of shame and guilt, sometimes even self-loathing."[14] The down side further brings a deeper separation of the spouses.

Pornography is a growing problem. Elder Dallin H. Oaks stated,

> A primary reason for the growing problem of pornography is that in today's world, words and images with sexual content and influences are everywhere: they can be found in movies, TV programs, social media, text messages, phone apps, advertisements, books, music, and everyday conversations. As a result, it is inevitable that all of us are being exposed to sexualized messages on a regular basis.[15]

President Gordon B. Hinckley stated,

> Pornography, with its sleazy filth, sweeps over the earth like a horrible, engulfing tide. It is poison. Do not watch it or read it. It will destroy you if you do. It will take from you your self-respect. It will rob you of a sense of the beauties of life. It will tear you down and pull you into a slough of evil thoughts and possibly of evil actions. Stay away from it. Shun it as you would a foul disease, for it is just as deadly. Be virtuous in thought and in deed. God has planted in you, for a purpose, a divine urge which may be easily subverted to evil and destructive ends.[16]

President Hinckley's statement brings to mind the true story of a mother who took her young children on a tour of the wooded area that surrounded their new home to acquaint them with the trees and vegetation. When they got to the poison ivy, she cautioned them not to touch it, as it would give them bumps that would itch and spread on their body. Her five-year-old son looked at it and questioned her warning in his mind.

After the tour was completed, he returned alone to look at the plant. He reached down and touched the plant a couple of times and saw no bumps on his finger. Next he grabbed a handful of the leaves and rubbed it on his arm and saw no bumps. Running to his mother, while rubbing the leaves on his arm, he told her she was wrong, and said, "See, no bumps." She grabbed him and ran into the house and tried all she could to wash away the juices of the plant. Too late. He got bumps everywhere on his arms, face, and body.

When the prophet says not to look at pornography or read it and to stay away from it, he knows what he's talking about. A person may not see the damage it can cause immediately, but it will come—and with a vengeance. Some men and women (young and old) question his word and think a little "touch" won't hurt. Just as he said, it pulls you in until it hooks you a little at a time. This is one of Satan's weapons to destroy you, your marriage, and your family. No wonder the prophet said to "shun it as you would a foul disease, for it is just as deadly."

The subversion that happens with pornography is that it puts someone else's body in place of the body of your mate. The natural urges that belong to your mate are directed at the unreal image or movie images. That which is meant to be enjoyed between husband and wife is done in a secret setting, causes the mind and body to think this is real, and gives that image control over your body. The scriptures put it this way: "And why wilt thou, my son, be ravished with a strange woman, and embrace the bosom of a stranger? For the ways of man are before the eyes of the Lord, and he pondereth all his goings. His own iniquities shall take the wicked himself, and he shall be holden with the cords of his sins."[17]

This description of "holden with the cords" is very true. Each viewing builds a reaction that grows stronger and stronger and harder to break, like being bound with cords. The body begins to crave more, and it takes more hard-core images and actions to satisfy the cravings. Such practice most often leads to seeking out different ways to gain satisfaction.

One person, highly successful in business, told how he would rent a motel room for four or five days and do nothing but watch pornography and masturbate. This behavior began to take a terrible toll on his marriage and business. He, like many, believed as long as he was alone and not at home, no one was harmed. The harm came from the hours spent away from his spouse, family, and work, and the practice of filling his mind with thoughts and images contrary to his covenants and the teachings of the Savior. His life was a perfect example of one "holden with the cords," which kept him from the marital happiness and business success he could have enjoyed.

Elder Russell M. Ballard observed,

> We see a rapid increase in cyberporn, involving sexual addiction over the Internet. Some become so addicted to viewing Internet pornography and participating in dangerous online chat rooms that they ignore their marriage covenants and family obligations and often put their employment at risk. Many run afoul of the law. Others develop a tolerance to their perverted behavior, taking ever more risks to feed their immoral addiction. Marriages crumble and relationships fail, as addicts often lose everything of real, eternal value.[18]

A spouse of a client reported that her husband, who has a six-figure salary, is so addicted to Internet pornography that he continues to risk viewing pornography at work even though warned. Businesses are becoming more aware of how pornography is damaging their employees' productivity and will not tolerate it. This person has lost sight of the risk of losing his income and the meaningful employment it affords, causing great concern for his wife. The viewing and the risk have put an almost fatal cloud over their marriage.

VIEWING CEASES TO BE ENOUGH

Each viewing of pornography leaves the viewer with the desire for more. It's the same as the drug addict, who finds each high is not as satisfying as the last and that it takes more drugs or stronger drugs to produce the same high. So it is with pornography. Then comes the time when viewing does not suffice. The Apostle Paul very effectively addressed this in his letter to the Galatians: "For the flesh lusteth against the Spirit, and the Spirit against the flesh: and these are contrary the one to the other: so that ye cannot do the things that ye would. . . . Now the works of the flesh are manifest, which are these; Adultery, fornication, uncleanness, lasciviousness."[19]

Much of pornography depicts those actions described by Paul. The viewer watches as objects interact in immoral behavior, and imagines him or herself in the middle of it all. There is no observing of caring or human feeling, just the satisfying lusts of the flesh. This objectifies the intimate relations with a spouse, creating an uncaring feeling and bringing about a less satisfying experience for both. For some, the watching becomes boring, and then the desire grows to act out with other people, who also become objects rather than true connections. The destruction of self and a marriage speeds on its downward spiral.

Kevin B. Skinner, PhD, reported:

> In a 2004 testimony before the United States Senate, Dr. Jill Manning shared some interesting data regarding pornography and relationships. In her research she found that 56 percent of divorce cases involved one party having an obsessive interest in pornographic websites. Another source, the American Academy of Matrimonial Lawyers, polled 350 divorce attorneys in 2003 where two-thirds of them reported that the Internet played a significant role in the divorces, with excessive interest in online porn contributing to more than half such cases.

He went on to report, "Every year for the past decade there have been roughly one million divorces in the United States. If half of the people divorcing claim pornography as the culprit, that means there are 500,000 marriages annually that are failing due to pornography."[20] No wonder the prophets have been warning us of the destructive nature of pornography.

OUR CHILDREN

The above statistics on divorce are alarming, as they represents families destroyed and children's lives affected. When pornography is in the home, our children are exposed to something they are not prepared to understand or deal with in a place that is supposed to be safe. Innocent exposure can be dealt with. However, to have the material in the home and see a parent or parents viewing it puts the child in a confusing dilemma, unable to understand what is right and what is wrong.

Some clients have reported that they thought their "adult material" was well hidden only to find the children discovered it. A few other clients reported that their children, as they got older, found the hidden files and saved links on the computer. The fortunate parents had their children show them what they found and asked what it meant. The unfortunate parents discovered their children took this as permission to do what the parent was doing.

One client reported her husband had a number of questionable movies he started watching with their older teenage boys, insisting they could handle the content. After awhile, the boys started treating their mother with much disrespect and rudeness and the husband simply said she was being too sensitive. That marriage ended in divorce, and the boys' lives were affected both by the loss of the marriage and the teaching of the father on how they should treat a wife and a mother. The effect continued as the boys grew and married and divorced.

Sister Linda S. Reeves, second counselor in the Relief Society General Presidency, stated,

> Many children, youth, and adults are innocently exposed to pornography, but a growing number of both men and women are choosing to view it and are drawn back repeatedly until it becomes an addiction. These individuals may desire with all of their hearts to get out of this trap but often cannot overcome it on their own. How grateful we are when these loved ones choose to confide in us as parents or a Church leader. We would be wise not to react with shock, anger, or rejection, which may cause them to be silent again.[21]

PROTECTING OUR FAMILY

Sister Reeves offered a solution to help our children:

> As we counsel with our children, together we can create a family plan with standards and boundaries,

being proactive to protect our homes with filters on electronic devices. Parents, are we aware that mobile devices with Internet capacity, not computers, are the biggest culprit? . . . How do we protect our children and youth? Filters are useful tools, but the greatest filter in the world, the only one that will ultimately work, is the personal internal filter that comes from a deep and abiding testimony of our Heavenly Father's love and our Savior's atoning sacrifice for each one of us.[22]

The far-reaching effect of pornography is recognized by other churches. For instance, in a twenty-two-page pastoral response to pornography, the United States Conference of Catholic Bishops stated, "Everyone, in some way, is affected by increased pornography use in society. We all suffer negative consequences from its distorted view of the human person and sexuality. As bishops, we are called to proclaim anew the abundant mercy and healing of God found in Jesus Christ, our Lord and Savior. . . ."[23]

WHAT IS THE SOLUTION?

In suggesting a solution to the problem of pornography, Elder Jeffery R. Holland said,

Above all, start by separating yourself from people, materials, and circumstances that will harm you. As those battling something like alcoholism know, the pull of proximity can be fatal. So too in moral matters. Like Joseph in the presence of Potiphar's wife, just run—run as far away as you can get from whatever or whoever it is that beguiles you. And please, when fleeing the scene of temptation, do not leave a forwarding address.[24]

When a person is exposed, the initial step to any solution has to be the recognition that there is a problem and that what we are now doing is not working. Because of volume of exposure, each person has to decide what influence it is having on his or her life as well as his or her response to the exposure. Any exposure to pornography is dangerous.

Often, denial has to be overcome. The one involved may think, "I don't have a problem, it is you that has the problem—you're overreacting." Sometimes it is hard to see the effect it is having on others. Once there is an awakening, another hurdle arises: discouragement. In the past, a victim was either involved or not involved and, if involved, he or she was automatically considered addicted. The first part of the statement is true while the second part needs clarification.

Elder Oaks gives a fresh look at the involvement question. He stated,

> In earlier times and circumstances, our counsel about pornography focused principally on helping individuals to avoid initial exposure or to recover from addiction. While those efforts are still important, past experience and current circumstances have shown the need for counsel addressed to levels of pornography use between the polar extremes of avoidance and addiction. . . . We also recognize that not everyone who uses pornography willfully is addicted to it. In fact, most young men and young women who struggle with pornography are not addicted.[25]

Elder Oaks introduces four different levels of individual involvement in pornography: (1) inadvertent exposure, (2) occasional use, (3) intensive use, and (4) compulsive use; only the fourth level is defined as addiction. The deeper the involvement, the harder it is to get out.

Elder Oaks makes an observation that is important for recovery. He states, "If behavior is incorrectly classified as an addiction, the user may think he or she has lost agency and the capacity to overcome the problem. This can weaken resolve to recover and repent. On the other hand, having a clearer understanding of the depth of a problem—that it may not be as ingrained or extreme as feared—can give hope and an increased capacity to exercise agency to discontinue and repent."[26]

Understanding the depth of the problem also helps those who are involved with the user—spouse, parents, and Church leaders. Such understanding recognizes the individual needs of each person. This clearer view spreads the encouragement of recovery to all. It also may help with the user's resolve to bring about a quicker and longer-lasting recovery.

In most of the recovery programs with the suffix of anonymous (such as alcoholics, sex, and gambling), the programs acknowledge the need for something outside of the individual. They call it a higher power. We recognize the higher power as that of the grace of our Savior, Jesus Christ and His Atonement. It is He that suffered for us in all things, and it is He who will help "after all we can do."[27] Each must choose to accept the Atonement as personal and meaningful in our own lives. We must accept His love and help, through which our own efforts become possible and our hearts become changed. As Elder Oaks states, "Any individual can escape the trap of pornography and fully recover, but this is possible only through drawing on the power of the Atonement."[28]

THINGS WE CAN DO

Behavior modification takes desire, commitment, and follow-through. It is not enough to just attempt to eliminate a behavior because all that does is leave a void that will try to get the old behavior back. It is imperative to develop a plan and actions to fill in the void.

Elder Oaks has outlined simple steps that will help develop a personal escape plan. He says it is important to recognize those happenings in life that are triggers to cravings. They can be stress, depression, loneliness, or feelings of worthlessness, to name a few. If we recognize the beginnings, then we can develop actions to withdraw from the temptations they bring. Each person needs an arsenal of actions. For instance, most viewing is done alone while shut up in a dark room; to protect yourself in this case, make sure you are with someone who loves you, out in the light. Make sure your computer or other electronics are out in the open. As we quoted Elder Holland above, you must separate yourself from that which draws you down.

Elder Oaks and Elder Holland each recommend refocusing our minds and action toward the Savior and His service. They tell us to fill our homes with art, music, and literature that bring the Spirit. In addition, regularly attend the temple and remember the tokens we take with us from the temple. Focus our thoughts. Picture in our minds our spouse and our children and our mothers. Such control takes responsibility for what we do with our minds and the thoughts we allow in it.

Sometimes in life, such as this one, we must be humble enough to seek additional help. Trust in the love of your spouse, your bishop, and a good therapist. They all can assist your journey to a full recovery and your attempt to once again feel the strength of the Spirit.

Spouses Can Be Significantly Helpful

Your marriage is worth saving, and every effort on the part of both husband and wife is vital. The love and faith of a spouse is priceless in the process of overcoming such an addiction. However, it can be a painful path for the innocent spouse, requiring righteous steadfastness in holding on through some extremely hard times. The comforting part is that the Savior will be with both of you.

In a Church magazine article, a woman told her story about her husband's addiction to pornography. She said, "When I discovered that my beloved eternal companion had become ensnared by pornography, I experienced the intense pain a wife in such a situation suffers. It is a deep sense of soul sickness, betrayal, and spiritual agony. . . . There is a sense of panic. The safety and peace of the marriage relationship evaporate. Trust, respect, honor, love, priesthood—all are deeply injured."

After much prayer and the continual pouring out of her heart to Heavenly Father, answers began to come. She told of her belief that their eternal marriage was precious to the Lord and that she knew He would be with them. She further realized "with great clarity that this was not my husband's problem alone. I could not, must not, passively stand by and hope he would conquer the problem by himself. I needed to be an active participant in this battle."

Her actions are an example for all who strive to help a mate through a serious problem. She told of times when the hurt resurfaced, requiring her to keep praying fervently. She said that during those times she made extra efforts to show her husband that her love for him was deep. "He needed to know we were a team and that together we would fight the enemy. His wife, his best friend, would stand by him. What a sweet experience it was for me to see his repentance process bringing light back into his life!"29

She is not alone in this struggle. Many could tell a similar story. Another Latter-day Saint woman whose husband overcame a pornography addiction said,

> In my darkest days, when I didn't know if my husband could find his way to the Atonement, I took

comfort from the story of the man with the palsy whose friends carried him to the Savior and lowered their sick friend into the home from the roof so Jesus could heal him (see Mark 2:1–12). I also remembered Alma the Younger, who in his youth apparently had no intention of repenting yet whose family continued to pray for him (see Mosiah 27:14). These two men found their way to repentance, healing, and happiness because of the faith of their family members and friends.

As she told of her own struggle of holding on with faith while her husband repented, she said that one day, after many years of facing this addiction struggle, she was at the temple, sitting in the chapel and silently thanking God for the progress their family had made. The organist was playing "Abide with Me; 'Tis Eventide," and the words of the hymn filled her mind and helped her realize how the Savior had stayed with her throughout her ordeal.

Then she added,

> Now, several years later, it is hard to remember the pain and almost impossible to feel it. . . . I don't remember all the awful things my husband said or did. . . . But I do remember what Alma taught about the Savior: "He will take upon him their infirmities, that his bowels may be filled with mercy, according to the flesh, that he may know according to the flesh how to succor his people according to their infirmities" (Alma 7:12). . . . [The Savior can] bring peace and joy to our hearts.[30]

The peace that comes from repentance is incalculable. Elder Allen D. Haynie of the Seventy said, "Repentance is real and it works. . . . It has the power to lift burdens and replace them with hope. It can lead to a mighty change of heart that results in our having 'no more disposition to do evil, but to do good continually' (Mosiah 5:2)."[31]

FINAL WORDS OF ENCOURAGEMENT

When we consider all the sorrow and heartache caused by pornography, we know that none of us wants it to be part of our lives. Safeguarding marriage by following the counsel of our Church leaders is a sure way to avoid it.

Elder Russell M. Nelson counseled:

> Marriage brings greater possibilities for happiness than does any other human relationship. Yet some married couples fall short of their full potential. They let their romance become rusty, take each other for granted, allow other interests or clouds of neglect to obscure the vision of what their marriage really could be. Marriages would be happier if nurtured more carefully.[32]

Nurture your marriage. Keep it pure and holy—and enjoyable. Avoid any activity that would diminish the love you have for each other, including even the slightest participation in anything pornographic.

In his March 2016 keynote address at the Utah Coalition Against Pornography Conference, Elder Jeffrey R. Holland renewed hope for anyone caught in this bondage. He said,

> Let me conclude by offering the basis for the hope I have; it is hope of the highest kind. I have deep, personal feelings for the atoning sacrifice of the Lord Jesus Christ and the power of his redemption. I declare that force, that pull, that saving grace to be infinite and eternal in its reach, a force and a grace that will save us from all kinds of bondage and lift all kinds of burdens if we but permit it, if we but seek it, and allow it into our lives. When hope is gone and lives are shattered in a hundred different ways for a thousand different reasons, the reality of Christ's redemptive, lifting, exalting power is still there.
>
> Against all odds and in spite of so much sin in the world, His promise is permanent, peaceful and everlasting.[33]

Notes

1. Gordon B. Hinckley, "A Tragic Evil among Us," *Ensign*, Nov. 2004.

2. Genesis 2:18; see also Moses 3:18.

3. Genesis 2:23; see also Moses 3:23.

4. Genesis 2:24; see also Moses, 3:24.

5. Spencer W. Kimball, *Teachings of Presidents of the Church: Spencer W. Kimball*, 200.

6. D&C 42:22.

7. Proverbs 5:18–19.

8. Ecclesiastes 9:9.

9. 1 Corinthians 7:3.

10. 1 Corinthians 7:4.

11. Ephesians 5:25.

12. Gordon B. Hinckley, *Teachings of Gordon B. Hinckley* (Salt Lake City: Deseret Book, 1997), 209.

13. Boyd K. Packer, "For Time and All Eternity," *Ensign*, Nov. 1993.

14. Mark Chamberlain, PhD, and Geoff Steurer, MS, LMFT, *Love You, Hate the Porn* (Salt Lake City: Shadow Mountain, 2011), 11–12.

15. Dallin H. Oaks, "Recovering from the Trap of Pornography," *Ensign*, Oct. 2015.

16. Gordon B. Hinckley, "Some Thoughts on Temples, Retention of Converts, and Missionary Service," *Ensign*, Nov. 1997.

17. Proverbs 5:20–22.

18. M. Russell Ballard, "Let Our Voices Be Heard," *Ensign*, Nov. 2003.

19. Galatians 5:17, 19.

20. Kevin B. Skinner, "Is Porn Really Destroying 500,000 Marriages Annually?" *Psychology Today*, Dec. 12, 2011, https://www.

psychologytoday.com/blog/inside-porn-addiction/201112/is-porn-really-destroying-500000-marriages-annually.

21. Linda S. Reeves, "Protection from Pornography—A Christ-Focused Home," *Ensign*, May 2014.

22. Ibid.

23. United States Conference of Catholic Bishops, "Create in Me a Clean Heart—A Pastoral Response to Pornography," ISBN 978-1-60137-527-8.

24. Jeffery R. Holland, "Place No More for the Enemy of My Soul," *Ensign*, May 2010.

25. Dallin H. Oaks, "Recovering from the Trap of Pornography," *Ensign*, Oct. 2015.

26. Ibid.

27. 2 Nephi 25:23.

28. Dallin H. Oaks, "Recovering from the Trap of Pornography," *Ensign*, Oct. 2015.

29. "My Husband's Addiction," *Liahona*, Aug. 2006.

30. "To the Tender Wives: What I Have Learned from my Husband's Addiction to Pornography," *Ensign*, Jul. 2013.

31. Elder Allen D. Haynie, "Remembering in Whom We Have Trusted," *Ensign*, Nov. 2015.

32. Russell M. Nelson, "Nurturing Marriage," *Ensign*, May 2006.

33. Mariah Proctor, "Elder Jeffrey R. Holland: Treat Pornography 'Like an Infectious, Fatal Epidemic,'" *Meridian Magazine*, Mar. 13, 2016, http://ldsmag.com/elder-jeffrey-r-holland-treat-pornography-like-a-infectious-fatal-epidemic/.

SAFEGUARD #9
Put Your Spouse before Your Children and Parents

*"Life's greatest partnership is in marriage—that relationship
which has lasting and eternal significance."*
—President Howard W. Hunter

PUTTING CHILDREN AND PARENTS BEFORE a spouse may be one of the most ignored temptations. Caring about loved ones is a good thing. Nonetheless, however much we love our family members, they must not take precedence over our spouse. Elder Russell M. Nelson made that clear when he said, "Let nothing in life take priority over your wife"[1]—and, of course, the same thing applies to your husband.

THE PLACE OF CHILDREN
The place of children on your priority list can be a hot-button topic because it's so easily misunderstood. Before you stand up and scream, "No one comes before my children!" take a minute and fully understand what is meant by putting your spouse before your children and why it matters.

First of all, it doesn't mean you don't love your children. Most parents cherish their children and would literally give their lives for them. Each child is vitally important to both parents and should be shown love unconditionally all his or her life. This isn't about not loving your children. It's about loving them enough to put your marriage—your spouse—first, knowing it will greatly enhance the security of your children.

In her article "Why My Husband Will Always Come Before My Kids," writer Amber Doty further emphasized this point when she said,

"There is no question that the bond between a mother and child is unbreakable. But I view my investment in my relationship with my spouse as one that is beneficial to our family as a whole. Prioritizing my husband's needs decreases our chances of getting divorced; it also increases the probability that our children will remain in a two-parent home."[2]

In blatant contrast to that thinking, we received an e-mail from a woman who had read one of our articles stating that a spouse needs to come before children. She was outraged and said, "My children will always come first! I can easily replace a husband—they're a dime a dozen. But I can never replace my children!" We were shocked by her cruel disregard for her husband. She needs to understand that while she may be able to replace her husband, she can never replace her children's father. Some may argue that a stepfather can fill the bill. We agree that there are some pretty amazing stepfathers, but there is only one father. Your children deserve a mother who honors their father.

When adorable little babies enter our lives, it's easy to turn our full attention to them. After all, they are helpless and need us to survive. And they are so cute! At one of our marriage seminars we were in conversation with a young father. He told us he and his wife had three little ones, all under the age of seven. We congratulated him on his family and smiled as we asked, "So are you still at the top of your wife's list?" His answer was not accompanied by a smile. He said, "Are you kidding? I'm not even on her list."

There are times in our lives when it seems difficult to keep our spouse at the top. One of these is when the children are young, as in the case of this young father. Kids place so many demands on our time. Nevertheless, the little things you do that make each other feel important need to be attended to. If they're not, life won't go nearly as well as it could.

WHEN YOU HAVE A SPECIAL-NEEDS CHILD

Keeping a spouse at the top of the list applies as well when a couple has a special-needs child. This child will likely require far more attention than your other children. If you are not careful, the child can take over the number-one spot on your list of priorities simply because of the special needs he or she may have. With this in mind, we'll share how two different couples handled their situation, each having given birth to a severely mentally and physically disabled child who requires constant care.

Case #1: Simon and Beverly's son Andy was born with several mental and physical disabilities. Both were deeply concerned and wanted to do all in their power to help their child. Beverly's motherly instincts went into overdrive. She felt driven to do everything for this child. Simon wanted to help, but Beverly felt only she could meet Andy's needs adequately. She gradually shut Simon out. Not only would she not allow him to help with their son, but she pushed him further and further away from having a close relationship with her. She made it clear that no room was left in her life for Simon.

Simon was devastated. He wanted to help, and he knew others— friends and family—wanted to help, also. Beverly would not accept help from anyone. Gradually he felt completely useless and only in the way. At one point he reached his limit and moved out. The couple eventually divorced.

Case #2: Curtis and Sylvia also had a son born with severe mental and physical disabilities. He required constant care, just as in the previous case. They also had three other children. Knowing the intense pressure this special-needs child would put on their marriage, Curtis and Sylvia made a decision. Sylvia said, "We knew that if our marriage were to survive, we had to put each other first. We had to work together and share the responsibility of not only our disabled child, but all of our children. We also knew that we couldn't do it on our own." They accepted help from their parents, other relatives, and friends, along with hiring help when needed.

They decided they would go out on a date once a week in order to focus only on each other and enjoy time together. She said, "This saved us. It was a time to laugh and have fun and reinforce our love for each other." They put their marriage first, all the while loving and caring for their children.

Their special-needs son passed away at the age of twenty-one, never having been able to walk, talk, or feed himself and all the while living at home with them. What he *could* do was smile. They loved his smile and happy countenance. It brought them shared joy amidst the hardship. When he was no longer with them, they were able to go forward and enjoy a happy life together because of the love they had nurtured for each other. In later years, their daughter said, "Mom and Dad were the ultimate love story. We loved it."

Children with varying degrees of needs exist. It may be a child with autism or any form of learning or physical disability. It may be a child who has made poor choices and is addicted to drugs. Any number of parenting challenges can arise that require special attention on the part of parents. No matter what the issues, as they are dealt with by the parents and child, the priority always remains the same. When your spouse is at the top of your list, your marriage will automatically be blessed. It's the proper order in the family. When you do respond to your spouse, it's like wrapping a warm cozy blanket around your children. It feels good—not only to the children, but to the couple. The marriage and the family feel safe when priorities are in place.

Years ago we attended a seminar by Dr. Carl Whitaker, a physician and pioneer in the field of psychotherapy. We were impressed with his wisdom and approach in helping families function at their highest level. His was the voice of not only learning, but of years of experience in counseling families. In his lecture that day he gave this rather shocking and profoundly important counsel: "In order for a family to work, the children must understand that the mother loves the father more than the children and that the father loves the mother more than the children." He then emphasized, "That doesn't mean they don't love their children. No. It just sets the proper order in the family. When that's in place, everything works much better."

The following story will show the power of this concept.

> A young college student shared [this] experience with us: "When I was little I used to ask my mom who she loved the most, me or Dad. She always said, 'Dad.' I asked him the same question, and he always answered 'Mom.' Of course, I knew they loved me, but I was always a little disappointed that they didn't say they loved me the most. A few years later I asked them again and the answer they gave showed me on top, at last. They each said they loved me the most."

Then she said, "The funny thing is, it didn't feel so good after all. It wasn't the feeling I was expecting. I liked it better when they said they loved each other the most." A few years later her parents were divorced. She said, "They needed to keep loving each other the most, then I might still have a mom and dad together."[3]

In an article titled "Message to My Kids: Mom Comes First," *New York Times* bestselling LDS author Jason F. Wright put it this way to his children: "I love you more than you know, maybe more than you'll ever know. Each of you is talented, kind, funny, and imperfect. All four of you are works-in-progress, just like your flawed folks. And you bring me and your mother more happiness than we can articulate.

"But never forget: Mom comes first."

He went on to explain that the kids are players on the team, and their mother is "our co-head coach, a full partner. Without her, this team would have a laughable, losing record." He then reminisced about a time when as a child he had been disrespectful to his mother. His dad was close enough, just around the corner, to hear the whole proceeding. In no time, his dad was at his side, putting his arm around him and gently teaching him a lesson he would not forget. But the most unforgettable part was what he saw a few minutes later—his dad sitting next to his sobbing mother with his arm around her. He said, "The image is unshakeable three decades later. They were a team.

"While I knew my dad loved me, I knew that my mother came first."

He ended the article by naming his children and saying, "I love you. But don't ever forget that no matter the day, the debate, the game or how much time is on the clock, Mom comes first."[4]

Ways Spouses Put Their Kids First and What to Do Instead

Here are some specifics so you can clearly see what you may be doing that puts your kids before your spouse. Most of these actions are small, simple, and easily overlooked.

Scenario #1: You're a stay-at-home mother of three. It's 6 p.m., the door opens, and you hear your husband say, "Hi, honey. I'm home." A minute earlier you heard your six-year-old son shout, "Mom, where's my soccer shirt? I can't find it anywhere!" At the same time your three-year-old is whining, "Read me a story, Mommy." To add to the chaos, the baby is crying. So when you hear "Honey, I'm home," you shout, "Thank goodness! Go find Richie's soccer shirt!"

You have just knocked your husband off the top and put the kids' needs first. That's not fair. He's been working hard all day, as have you. We suggest you stick the pacifier in the baby's mouth, put the soccer shirt and story on hold, and make a beeline for your husband. But first respond by saying something like, "Hooray! You're home." That way he knows where you are and can meet you as you hurry to him.

Put your arms around him and plant a kiss on his lips. Not a peck. A kiss—the kind that lets him know without a doubt that you are happy beyond words to be with him again. Then enjoy being in each other's arms for a minute or two.

If you do this, three things will happen. First, he'll know he's number one on your list and you'll know you're top on his; second, the kids will know their parents love each other; and third, it will fill you both with the emotional energy to go forth and meet the needs of the family.

If you think your kids are not watching, think again. Here's an excerpt from a letter twin sisters attending college away from home wrote to their younger siblings. They and their parents gave us permission to share it. These coeds were giving their sisters advice on finding a future mate. They wrote: "Dreams come true and you have to dream big. Tonight when Dad comes home from work or meetings, listen to the first words he'll say when he walks in the door: 'Where's my beautiful wife?' Then watch as he searches the house to find her, just so he can kiss her to let her know he loves her. Notice how he'll start helping with whatever he can right away, and how he makes every one of you feel so important as he asks about your day. Pay attention to the way he really listens. . . . You can have someone like that, and you deserve someone like that."[5]

Oh, yes. Your kids are watching. They are either learning how to keep their future spouse on the top of the list while loving the kids, or they are observing how not to.

Scenario #2: It's dinnertime. Your wife has worked hard cooking a special meal. Everyone is hungry, including you. You and the kids quickly take your places at the table. Your wife is still busy in the kitchen, bringing in the last part of the meal. Finally, exhausted, she takes her seat and everyone begins to chow down. To your kids, your wife seems to be little more than hired help. She cooks. They eat. Not fair.

Consider this option instead. When you come home, you smell the aroma of a delicious meal wafting through the house. You go to the kitchen, greet your wife with a kiss, then say, "Smells good, honey. What can I do to help?" The kids are hungry and eager to eat and have run to sit at the table. You take a moment and say to them, "Hey, kids. Mom has worked hard fixing dinner. Let's help her." Then you say to your wife, "How about we have Jimmy put the water in the glasses? Would it help if Janie put the rolls and butter on?" Then you pitch in and help. They hear you thank her for working hard to make such a delicious meal for them and you. The children see you showing respect to your wife. They see that her needs matter more to you than your own or theirs. They get the picture—Mom comes first.

Scenario #3: It's your wedding anniversary. It's also Billie's little league game—no playoff, just a regular game. Both you and your wife have enjoyed going to these weekly games and giving your support to your son. So you say to your wife, "We can't let Billie down. We need to be at his game." She was hoping you could go out and celebrate your anniversary together, just the two of you. But, nope. The kid came first.

Here's the point: Kids don't always need to come first. In real life, they will find out that things will not always go their way. It's a good lesson to learn. It's not like you are abandoning your child if you miss a game now and then for something important to you or your spouse.

So you take a moment, preferably at least a day before the event, sit down with the kids, and explain, "Mom and I were married on this date twelve years ago. This is a very special day for us—it's our anniversary. To show my love for Mom, I'm taking her out for a special date. We won't be at your game this time, but we're sure you'll have a good time anyway. This is a very important celebration for us. I hope you'll kiss your mom and wish her happy anniversary. And, since it's my anniversary as well, how about giving me a big hug, too."

Scenario #4: Your husband comes home looking more tired than usual. You can tell he's had a "no good very bad" day. You may be thinking, *He's not the only one who's had a bad day. I could use a little help right now.* Instead, on this day when you can see his needs are greater than usual, you decide to focus on him for a few minutes. You can see he needs a little time to wind down. After you greet him with a loving kiss, you take his coat and invite him to sit in his easy chair. You may even bring him a glass of apple juice (or whatever drink you know he likes). Some days a husband just needs this kind of special attention. You tell the kids to give Dad a few minutes to relax. They see that his well-being matters to you. They plainly see that Dad comes first.

OTHER SIMPLE WAYS TO PUT YOUR SPOUSE BEFORE YOUR KIDS

Scenario #1: The family is all seated at the table, the blessing on the food has been said, and it's time to dig in. The wife takes the meat plate and passes it to her husband, saying, "Dad gets first pick." No question. Dad is number-one to Mom. He thanks her, smiles, and says, "You first, honey." It's obvious they respect and love each other.

Scenario #2: Everyone is heading out the door for a family outing. The kids run out and jump into the car. They're excited to go. As Mom and Dad reach the car, they notice that Dad walks around to Mom's side and opens the car door for her. They hear her thank him for it. It's one way their son learns to respect his future wife, or how their daughter learns to allow her future husband to respect her.

Scenario #3: It's a cold winter day, and the family has gone out to eat at a nice restaurant. As the kids take their seats, they see Dad helping Mom remove her coat and place it over the back of her chair. Then they see Dad pull Mom's chair out as she takes her seat. It feels good to see how kindly their dad treats their mom. They can easily tell that she is top on his list.

Scenario #4: It's Friday night—your regular date night. You both know how important this night is. It's a time to be together without the kids and pressures of anything else. Going on these dates shows that your marriage is important, that it needs to be kept fresh and fun.

An illustration of the importance of having a date night happened when a couple called their married son one Friday evening. Their son's fifteen-year-old daughter answered the phone. After a short greeting, they asked to speak to her dad. "Oh, he's not here. Mom and Dad are out on their weekly date. I'm babysitting." It's a wise couple who put their spouse first by going on these kinds of dates regularly. It shows the kids that their parents cherish time alone together.

Kids don't have to go everywhere with the parents. It's good for them to hear Dad say, "I'm taking Mom on a date. Be good. We'll see you when we get home. Don't call us unless there's an emergency." Then, as he puts his arm around his wife and they walk out, it's like that warm, cozy security blanket is wrapped around the kids again. Mom and Dad are putting each other first.

Speakers Pam and Bill Farrel put it this way: "It's vital, every day, to carve out time out of earshot of the kids. Additional time together each week, as well as monthly and yearly getaways, will help remind both of you why you first fell in love."[6]

We agree. Besides those weekly dates, take an occasional overnighter to a nice hotel. Spoil each other. Let your spouse know he or she is your first priority.

Hundreds of other scenarios in a couple's everyday life show how to honor, respect, and love each other—how to be each other's number one. Think how you may be able to improve in your own effort to make sure the message is loud and clear that "Mom comes first" and "Dad comes first." That's a great example for kids to see.

A CAUTION FOR BLENDED FAMILIES

Blending a family can be tricky, to say the least. When couples divorce they do not divorce their children—they divorce only their children's father or mother. When they remarry, an automatic loyalty to the new stepparent generally doesn't happen. Experience shows that it takes about seven years for a true blending to take place. Sometimes it takes much longer, and sometimes it never seems to happen at all.

Remember, your kids are used to seeing you with their own parent, not a new love in your life. That's a bitter pill for most children to swallow. This is a subject that could fill a whole book. However, in an effort to clarify how keeping your new spouse as your priority while still showing appropriate love for your children, here are a few ideas to consider.

During your courtship with your soon-to-be new spouse, talk about where the children fit. Let your intended know how important your children are to you. Talk about ways you can show your love to your children while still keeping each other as your most important priority.

Do not be jealous of time your new spouse spends with his or her children. They need to have times when they can talk freely to their parent without having to guard every word or be afraid of offending the stepparent. That does not mean the parent will allow his new spouse to be bashed by his kids. Respect must be taught while still listening to the child's concerns. While most conversations can and should be to both the parent and stepparent, some alone time with a parent is important.

The potential danger here is when the parent spends too much time with his or her children without the new spouse. That can cause a huge rift in the marriage. Tom and Milly had this problem. Tom spent many hours visiting with his married daughter, Jana, without Milly being present. Jana was used to having her father all to herself and wasn't at all happy to relinquish the number-one spot she had played in his life since her parents' divorce.

Tom had to learn how to keep his new wife as his priority while still keeping a good relationship with his daughter. He needed to openly discuss his priorities with his daughter and his new wife. It was hard telling Jana that his top priority was now Milly, but he made it clear that he wanted to spend time with Jana when she needed some alone time with her dad, but that mostly he wanted to include Milly so she would have the chance to grow close to Jana.

Next came the task of convincing Milly that his being alone with Jana on some occasions did not mean he loved Milly any less. If Jana had been demanding and belligerent to her father in this new situation, she would have needed to be reminded that he loved her, but he now had a new wife and would be doing all in his power to build a happy marriage with her, without excluding Jana from his life. Through it all he insisted that Jana treat Milly with respect.

He needed to ask Milly to be patient while Jana came to grips with this new reality. He promised Milly that in all his associations with Jana he would show loving respect to Milly. He asked her to treat Jana with this same kind of respect.

Stepparents need to feel they are number one in their new spouse's life, and yet be accepting of the love that is needed from the biological parent to his or her children. This works as well when both spouses come into the marriage with children. It can be complicated when both husband and wife are now stepparents. The application is the same.

The real tragedy comes when the divorced spouse tries to turn the children against their former mate's new spouse. This can cause nothing but confusion and grief in the lives of the children. If you are divorced, don't do this.

The best possible scenario is for all concerned to build kind and caring relationships. It simply takes time and a lot of compassionate effort and understanding. The foundation is keeping your new spouse as your number-one priority while still loving and paying attention to your children.

WHEN CHILDREN RULE, THEY AND SOCIETY SUFFER

Far too many children in today's world think they come before everyone else. They somehow believe they are privileged and deserve the number-one spot—at all cost. This breeds a selfish generation of people who care mostly for themselves and their own wants and needs. This attitude of entitlement will not bode well for your children or for society. We need adults who care for others, not just themselves. If you make sure your children do not grow up in a household where everything revolves around them, your children will be prepared to face the real world with far more confidence and ability. All aspects of their lives will be enriched as a result.

When children grow up in a home where the parents put each other before the children, they are better equipped to face reality. Of course, they also need to grow up knowing they were deeply loved and respected by their parents.

When you know you're number one in your mate's life, all else falls into place.

As a result, you will have more time and energy to devote to other important matters, the most important of these being the care of your children.

It's Back to Just Two

Kids grow up. They move out and start their own lives. The more quickly that happens when they are young adults, the better life is for them and their parents. Hopefully you have shown them the way to find their own happiness as adults. When this happens, as it should, it's back to just the two of you. It's like the beginning, only better, because of all you've been through that has cemented your love for each other.

Some couples struggle during this period of their lives. Some even divorce after forty-plus years of being together. That's a sad outcome when this stage of marriage is bursting with opportunities for fulfillment.

One of the problems here is that one spouse or the other is not willing to let the kids go. They're still putting the kids first, above their spouse. They feel compelled to still be an integral part of their children's lives. It's important to realize that you will not be the center of the universe for your children. Maybe you were when they were very young, but no longer. Now they have their own lives. They *need* to have their own lives. And you need to have yours. Keeping your spouse as a priority over the kids will help make that happen. It will be easier if you've done it all along throughout the years of their growing up.

To keep yourselves in that number-one spot in your marriage, consider backing up to how it was when you first fell in love. From the *Courier Journal* came this wise counsel: "Act like you're dating. Couples often become complacent after many years of marriage. They may forget about the little details that made the relationship fun in the early years. The personal notes and cards and other surprises may fall by the wayside after being together for some time. Make an effort to go on dates, write love notes and think of what was appreciated by your partners when you were in the dating stage."7 These are the little acts that let your spouse know he or she comes first.

President Spencer W. Kimball reminded us, "Love is like a flower, and, like the body, it needs constant feeding. The mortal body would soon be emaciated and die if there were not frequent feedings. The tender flower would wither and die without food and water. And so love, also, cannot be expected to last forever unless it is continually fed with portions of love, the manifestation of esteem and admiration, the expressions of gratitude, and the consideration of unselfishness."8

The later years, when kids are grown and gone, can be sweet and filled with love. Of course, you'll still love and enjoy being with your children, which, if you've built a strong marriage, will be a joyful sharing of being grandparents.

Reality reminds us that these years may also be fraught with illness. That's when peace comes by having that mate by your side, knowing from past experience that he or she will do all in their power to take good care of you. You will likely have the chance to care for each other throughout these later years. When your children see you caring for each other, always putting each other first, they will see how important it has been all along for Mom to love Dad most and for Dad to love Mom most. This is a marital legacy filled with love and devotion—a great gift to give to your posterity.

Now About Your Parents

Now that we've put children in their proper place, it's time to consider your parents. No one should come before your spouse—not even Mom or Dad. Some wives and husbands think their devotion lies first with their parents. This is wrong thinking. In order for your marriage to grow and flourish, you must put your mate first. Such concern is not being disloyal to your parents. You still love and respect them, it's just that your spouse comes first.

We are told in scripture, "Therefore shall a man leave his father and his mother, and shall cleave unto his wife: and they shall be one flesh."[9] Regarding this we quote from a site dedicated to answering biblical questions that stated:

> This indicates that in a family there are two types of relationships. The parent-child relationship is the temporary one and there will be a "leaving." The husband-wife relationship is the permanent one—"what God has joined together, let man not separate" (Matthew 19:6). Problems occur in family life when these two roles are reversed and the parent-child relationship is treated as the primary relationship. When an adult child has married and this parent-child relationship remains primary, the newly formed union is threatened.[10]

Regarding the couple's relationship with their parents, here are a couple of tips on how you can keep your spouse as your number-one priority.

When something wonderful happens in your life, your spouse needs to be the first to know. When you get a promotion, let your wife or husband be the first call to hear the news. The same is true when you experience disappointment. Let your spouse hear it from you, not from a secondary source. It's hurtful when your spouse's parent calls you to discuss the good or sad news that you know nothing about.

When your parent needs your help at the same time your spouse needs it, what then? It's simple—take care of your spouse, then your parent. If your parent's need is urgent, then of course you will respond, but only after explaining the need to your spouse. In all things you will first consider the needs and feelings of your spouse. Sometimes you can call on others to help meet the needs of your parents. The bottom line is, do not make a habit of neglecting your spouse in favor of your parents.

HOW WE HONOR OUR PARENTS AS ADULTS

There are many ways to show respect to your parents. The loving relationship you have with them need never be diminished by your devotion to your wife or husband. That being said, parents need their adult children to care about them. This need grows as they enter their declining years. Couples need to discuss ways they can cherish and care for their parents without overpowering their relationship with each other.

Sally and Nathan were faced with the challenge of his aging mother. She was becoming senile and complained endlessly about her aches and pains, which were mostly legitimate. She was unwilling to do even small tasks for herself. They set up a plan with his two siblings to help out on certain days. Too many times the siblings failed to do their part, and the duty fell back on Sally, the only one who was not employed at the time. Nathan seemed somewhat oblivious to how this was affecting his wife.

Sally began to feel resentment toward Nathan for not being more concerned about her well-being than his mother's. He and the rest of the family were relying on her too much. Sally and Nathan had a serious talk about what needed to be done. He realized that his wife was suffering from carrying the heavy load of his mother's care, which at times included lifting her. It became more than Sally could bear, physically and emotionally. After meeting with his siblings, it was decided his mother needed to be in a care center where twenty-four-hour care could be given. His mother now has the care she needs and Sally has become his first priority, as she should be.

Adult children sometimes get confused about how to honor their parents. The best way you can honor them is to emulate the good teachings they gave you as a child. Becoming a good spouse and parent to your own children is one of the best ways you can honor your parents. They want your happiness more than anything. Help them as you can, but do not allow them to take over your lives.

THE FINAL WORD
Regarding the place of our spouse, President Spencer W. Kimball reminds us of what the scripture means when he said,

> The Lord says in no uncertain terms: "Thou shalt love thy wife with all thy heart, and shall cleave unto her and none else" (D&C 42:22). . . .
>
> The words *none else* eliminate everyone and everything. The spouse then becomes preeminent in the life of the husband or wife, and neither social life nor occupational life nor political life nor any other interest nor person nor thing shall ever take precedence over the companion spouse.[11]

These words of counsel from a prophet clearly let us know that children and parents must not take precedence over your spouse. Keeping this in mind will help safeguard your marriage.

Notes
1. Russell M. Nelson, "Our Sacred Duty to Honor Women," *Ensign*, May 1999.
2. Amber Doty, "Why My Husband Will Always Come Before My Kids," *Huffington Post*, Apr. 16, 2015, http://www.huffingtonpost.

com/yourtango/why-my-husband-will-always-come-before-my-kids_b_7033384.html.

3. Gary and Joy Lundberg, "10 Ways You Are Being Unfaithful to Your Spouse, and Don't Even Know It," *Meridian Magazine*, Oct. 18, 2014, http://ldsmag.com/article-1-15019/.

4. Jason F. Wright, "Wright Words: Message to My Kids: Mom comes first," *Deseret News*, Jan. 13, 2015, http://www.deseretnews.com/article/865619455/Message-to-my-kids-Mom-comes-first.html.

5. CaMarie Hoffman, "Letter to Our Sisters: Someone Who Loves You Like Dad Loves Mom," *All Boys But 9*, Oct. 1, 2014, http://www.allboysbut9.com/someone-who-loves-you-like-dad-loves-mom/#.WJx_q_krK70.

6. Pam and Bill Farrel, "How to Keep Your Marriage Strong during Life Transitions," *Focus on the Family*, 2014, http://www.thrivingfamily.com/Features/Magazine/2014/how-to-keep-your-marriage-strong-during-life-transitions.aspx.

7. "Keeping Marriage Going Strong into Your Golden Years," *Courier Journal*, Aug. 27, 2013.

8. Spencer W. Kimball, *Marriage and Divorce* (Salt Lake City: Deseret Book Co., 1976), 22–23.

9. Genesis 2:24.

10. "How do you balance leave and cleave with honoring your parents?" *Got Questions?* http://www.gotquestions.org/leave-cleave-honor.html.

11. Spencer W. Kimball, *Teachings of President of the Church: Spencer W. Kimball*, 199.

SAFEGUARD #10
Put Your Spouse before Your Career and Church Work

"Let the husband render unto the wife due benevolence:
and likewise also the wife unto the husband."
—1 Corinthians 7:3

SCRIPTURES ARE MEANT TO WAKE us up and focus us on greater truths. So it is with the scripture from Genesis and Moses we have already quoted concerning leaving mother and father, cleaving to your wife, and becoming one flesh. President Spencer W. Kimball said, "Do you note that? She, the woman, occupies the first place. She is preeminent."[1]

Marriage is a delicate balance dealing with two lives that are usually out of balance most of the time. Having everything in balance at all times is an impossible dream. When we married, we did so with the expectation of finding and building happiness. We were not sure how to get that happiness, and we knew it came with a price.

President Spencer W. Kimball answers the question, "What is the price of happiness?" He states,

> You will be surprised with the simplicity of the answer. The treasure house of happiness may be unlocked and remain open to those who use the following keys: First, you must live the gospel of Jesus Christ in its purity and simplicity—not a half-hearted compliance, but hewing to the line, and this means an all-out devoted consecration to the great program of salvation and exaltation in an orthodox manner. Second, you must forget yourself and love your companion more

than yourself. If you do these things, happiness will be yours in great and never failing abundance.[2]

These two steps bring balance to our lives. It is the strength of the Savior and the gospel and the knowledge that our mate is there, steady and strong, that gives us that special unvarying something to hold to. It is the sure foundation we stand on so when the adversary "shall send forth his mighty winds, yea, his shafts in the whirlwind, yea, when all his hail and his mighty storm shall beat upon you," we have the promise, "it shall have no power over you to drag you down to the gulf of misery and endless wo, because of the rock upon which ye are built, which is a sure foundation, a foundation whereon if men build they cannot fall."[3]

Years ago, during a discussion on courtship, the instructor emphasized that one very important question needs to continually be asked: "How do I feel about me when I am with you?" The importance of this question stays throughout married life. The answer conveys how important I believe I am to you, my spouse. It isn't how you intend to have me feel—it is how I actually feel. Along with this question couples need to ask, "How do you feel about us when we are apart?" We cannot control how the other person feels; however, we can help how they feel.

Becoming one flesh, rendering benevolence, and cleaving to none else has to do with the feelings spouses experience with each other. The belief of the preeminent position comes from the actions that surround the execution of the above scriptural words. With this said, demands of living enter marital life, two of which are the need to earn a living and the need to serve the Lord in Church callings (fully living the gospel). In both of these categories, the scripture from Ecclesiastes is applicable: "To every thing there is a season, and a time to every purpose under the heaven. . . . For a man to rejoice, and to do good in his life. And also that every man should eat and drink, and enjoy the good of all his labour, it is the gift of God."[4]

EARNING A LIVING

The ways of earning a living are many and diverse. They vary also with the time of life we're in. What we do in the beginning of our employment life is different from later in life. As knowledge and experience are gained, so are different opportunities opened up. A desire to earn more money and to have a chance to influence the success of a business usually grows.

This progression often comes at a price in more time, more training, or more education. In reality, all three of these are needed. Career paths used to be more clear. Often a person would stay at the same company throughout an entire working career. Now, working is like a game of chess, and people make strategic moves to gain advantage for personal desires, more opportunities, a chance for greater earnings, and more recognition of skills.

Again, what is the price paid in this progress? Some, like Craig, joined a company and had the personality, skills, and work ethic to progress quickly up the business ladder. His progression in earning money and prestige came so fast that he became completely convinced of his own importance. He believed he had outgrown his basic beliefs, virtues, and even his family. Craig partied with the big boys and began to live their lifestyle. Like many of those "big boys," in time the world took over and he became lost to alcohol, drugs, and immorality. He ended up losing all that he had. Many examples of this very journey flourish in all walks of life in big business, small business, sports—you name the career and you can see the example.

Beth, a talented performer, found working and being involved in the arts more fulfilling than being a mother and wife. As success grew, she spent more time and energy away and had less time and desire to be with her family. Eventually she moved out from the family and divorce ensued, leaving in its wake a husband and children filled with hurt, abandonment, anger, loneliness, and confusion.

It isn't always success that changes a person. Lack of success brings the discouragement, depression, and frantic reaching for some kind of quick relief often found in drugs, alcohol, pornography, and immorality. All are selfish in nature and put emphasis on self only. These same pressures and feelings are felt by your spouse and need to be addressed together. When joint commitment to spouse, marriage, family, and gospel principles are in your life, then all of these can be faced together with the strength of each other.

Sometimes when our marriage or our family is a little more challenging or hard, we look for a way to escape that can be seem justified—or at least that appears to be so. This is called the unassailable position. You spend more time at work to do busyness, unnecessary jobs, or to shoot the breeze. All the time you are able to say to yourself or your spouse, "I'm here earning our living"—or in case of Church work, "I'm here serving the Lord." How can anyone question these noble purposes? Rather than face the things that need to be faced, we look for a place to hide. Oops, just got found out!

There are times when work, schooling, or even Church work put life out of balance out of necessity. Business trips, specialized training, military deployment, long study sessions, a doctor doing residency, or in our case eighteen months apart to get an advanced degree are examples of difficult but normal happenings. How do we choose to handle these occurrences? Some handle them better than others.

Here's what we did during that eighteen-month separation time. Joy stayed with our children at home while I stayed with my brother and his wife more than six hundred miles away to work on my degree. Money was tight, to say the least, as we paid for schooling needs. Joy worked from home as a writer to bring in some added income. I also held a part-time job that worked with my school schedule. This was before cell phones, and every call was expensive except those made after eleven p.m. We decided that's when we would call twice a week and talk for one hour, rather than making several short calls during the day. We also decided we would find a way to see each other every other month. I would drive home or she would drive to see me. It was a difficult time, but our plan worked and helped us stay close. Finally, I graduated with my degree in marriage and family therapy. I was successful right out of the chute: I got a family back together—us!

Later, when I decided I wanted to share what I'd learned by becoming a professional speaker, I faced another decision. I joined the state branch of a national organization. I met with local people who were involved in the same pursuit and attended three national conventions, rubbing shoulders with talented, motivated, and highly successful speakers. At each convention, I not only listened to their presentations, I got to know them on a more personal level and was shocked to find out that a very high percentage of them were divorced. When I returned home, I discussed this with my wife and what this might mean to our marriage. Together we decided that if we wanted to be on any speaking circuit, we would do it together or not at all. That's when we began speaking together. Our youngest son had left on a mission, and we were in a position to travel without leaving any children behind.

Our plan worked for us, but it may not work for you. Every couple needs to decide what will work for them. The needs and desires of each will need to be considered as you decide how to plot a course that will strengthen, not diminish, your marriage while you still earn a living.

Tim, a successful business executive, found himself gone more and more as he progressed in his company. As he was driving on a trip, he thought about his wife, and a knot in his stomach formed as he replayed in his mind his wife's statement: "Tim, I feel like a single parent." About that time, he heard Dr. James Dobson of Focus on the Family saying on the radio, "Men, if your career is causing you to miss out on your family, you need to pray and ask God to provide you a job where you can be a true husband to your wife and a good father to your children." In his mind, Tim said, "That is me. I know about faith and I know about prayer and I know I'm missing out on my family." Inspiration comes at different times and in different ways. Tim started looking for a different job, found one that allowed him to be at home more, and it turned out to be more satisfying work.[5]

It takes both spouses to keep each other first. Michelle, the wife of Ron, a young doctor, decided she needed to be available with their baby and a toddler during the time her husband had lunch on some of his long days of internship at the hospital. She planned times to be in the cafeteria with their young children so they could have a meal as a family. She often had to wait a couple of hours until he had a break and could run in and join them. He had no way of knowing when his breaks would be; his mealtime could not be scheduled. Her efforts helped keep them close during this difficult time. She wasn't the only one working at keeping their relationship strong. Ron called her whenever he had a micro minute to say, "No time to talk, but just want you to know I am thinking of you and I love you."

The point we're making here is to look at your career path and see if it's compatible with creating a happy marriage. It's true, sacrifices will have to be made along the way, but even then couples need to do all they can to put each other first. No amount of climbing your career ladder will compensate for losing your marriage.

Some couples face hard choices when their income requires the husband to take two jobs so his wife can stay home with the children. When that happens, couples must work doubly hard to find time for each other. Fitting in small moments to connect can make all the difference. Negotiating together to discover ways this can be done will pay off. Pray for help to know how to do this.

We are reminded of a couple who faced a similar problem. His income was not sufficient to cover the expenses of their growing family. The wife was about to succumb and look for a job to help out, knowing that her children would need a babysitter, but the couple couldn't see a way out. That's when an inspired visiting teacher presented a plan to them.

She said, "Figure out how much more you need a month in actual dollars to make ends meet comfortably. Then pray together as a couple and tell the Lord that's how much you need. Be specific in the exact amount needed. Let Him know your desires to stay home with your little ones and for your husband to have time with his family, too. Be specific in your prayers. Then fast and keep praying that your husband will either get a raise in that amount or a new job will come along to meet the need."

They did as she suggested. To their delight, within a few weeks he was offered a promotion at work that provided the exact amount they needed. Sometimes we forget to be specific in our requests for the Lord's help. The scriptures remind us that "ye have not because ye ask not."[6] We need to work hard and continually ask for the Lord's help in providing for our family His way. That way your needs are met and your marriage is protected.

SERVICE TO THE LORD
Part of being committed and active in the Church means opportunities to serve in many different capacities. Some callings are more time-consuming than others. From bishop to auxiliary presidents, counselors, secretaries, teachers, Scoutmasters, compassionate service leaders, home and visiting teachers, and the myriad of volunteer services performed, untold hours of dedicated service are given. All of this service to the Lord functions if, as President Kimball said, we are "all out devoted" to the plan of salvation. However, this advice needs to be balanced

with the statement of President David O. McKay, who said, "No other success can compensate for failure in the home."7

In many homes the balance is handled well, due to the overall feeling of love and preeminence and importance of spouse to spouse. This balance allows for a joint desire and commitment to serve family and others. This belief and feeling allows for spurts of unbalanced time commitment when needed to fulfill an assignment or need.

Years ago, we, along with Douglas and Janice Kapp Perry, wrote and produced an LDS musical production, "It's a Miracle," to promote missionary service. The talented woman who played the mother was a mother of ten children. We performed the production 239 times over nearly four years throughout the United States, and she appeared in 200 of the 239 performances. Though young children were at home, her husband told us that because of his wife's dedication to him and the family throughout the years of their marriage, she needed this opportunity to use her great talent and do a service to strengthen members of the Church. We have observed this same attitude as both of them have served in many Church callings and in civic opportunities. They have focused on the development of each other's talents and desires, each sacrificing at times for the other. In so doing, they have built a strong marriage.

In our travels within the U.S. and in a number of foreign countries, we have seen the many hours of mutually supported service of wonderful couples. Such service often earns a fun title given to a spouse—things like "Brother Relief Society" (the husband of the Relief Society president) or "Sister Bishop" (the wife of the bishop, whose last name is *not* Bishop). These titles are affectionately given to the mate for the willing and positive help shown.

Sometimes the spurts are not spurts, and the feeling of being number one to a spouse is lost. For instance, a client remarked, "The whole ward loves my husband because he will fix anything for anybody at any time; all the while, our home remodeling projects have been left mostly undone." Or the husband who remarked, "My wife is a great cook and everybody loves her cooking—which we don't get to have much of at home." As mates, our focus is lost, "Because [our] hearts are set so much upon the things of this world, and aspire to the honors of men [and women]"8 that we neglect taking care of home. Service is not an either/or principle; it is an "and" principle—mate and others, not just others.

This brings up another thought. Maybe as mates we neglect honoring the service given to and for each other. Many clients remark they do not believe they are appreciated for what they do, but are only reminded where they fall short. The answer to this is simple. Focus on the good things your mate does and use liberally what we learned in Primary: say "Thank you."

Accepting callings is important to keeping our covenants. Often through this service we learn how to love and honor our spouses. Only when the service gets out of balance and is allowed to take precedence over our spouse do we get into trouble.

SERVICE ENHANCES OUR MARRIAGE

As we court and then marry, we work together to decide the philosophy that will guide our life together. When we marry in the temple, we seek the Lord's blessing and sealing power upon our union. The scriptures give us an idea of how to make our house the Lord's way: "Organize yourselves; prepare every needful thing; and establish a house, even a house of prayer, a house of fasting, a house of faith, a house of learning, a house of glory, a house of order, a house of God."9

It is interesting that the scripture tells us to "prepare every needful thing," which includes a place to live, furnishings, and a way to pay for our life together—things needed to establish a house. Then we find the instructions on the spiritual necessities to have a house of God. With all of this comes the need to make a choice of actively serving. Together as a couple we need to overtly make the statement, "Choose you this day whom ye will serve . . . but as for me and my house, we will serve the Lord."10

Service broadens married life and opens a way to find friends with similar desires and commitment. All of this has to be done as a joint resolution to keep your mate in the preeminent number-one position.

DUE BENEVOLENCE

To *show forth due benevolence* means to have a disposition to do good and do acts of kindness, goodwill, and charitableness with a desire to promote the other's happiness. That is what marriage is all about—promoting each other's happiness. The Savior told us, "Thou shalt love thy neighbour as thyself."[11] Your closest neighbor is your mate. We learned a universal truth from a man much younger than we. He said, "I can expect nothing more of someone else than I am willing to give." When we mutually treat our spouse as preeminent number one, we get the same treatment back—love and respect.

President Gordon B. Hinckley puts an exclamation point on this chapter with this comment: "I am satisfied that happiness in marriage is not so much a matter of romance as it is an anxious concern for the comfort and well-being of one's companion. Any man who will make his wife's comfort his first concern will stay in love with her throughout their lives and through the eternity yet to come"[12] This is equally true for a wife regarding her husband.

Notes

1. Spencer W. Kimball, "The Blessings and Responsibilities of Womanhood," *Ensign*, Mar. 1976.

2. Spencer W. Kimball, *Faith Precedes the Miracle* (Salt Lake City: Bookcraft, 1973), 126.

3. Helaman 5:12.

4. Ecclesiastes 3:1, 12–13.

5. Chuck Holton, "Becoming a Family Man," *Focus on the Family*, 2003, http://www.focusonthefamily.com/parenting/parenting-roles/the-involved-father/family-man.

6. James 4:2.

7. *Doctrine and Covenants and Church History Student Study Guide*, 2005, 199; https://www.lds.org/manual/doctrine-and-covenants-and-church-history-student-study-guide/the-worldwide-church/president-david-o-mckay-no-other-success-can-compensate-for-failure-in-the-home?lang=eng.

8. D&C 121:35.

9. D&C 88:119.

10. Joshua 24:15.

11. Matthew 22:39.

12. Gordon B. Hinckley, Anchorage, Alaska, Regional Conference, June 18, 1995.

SAFEGUARD #11
Be Willing to Forgive Your Spouse

*"Heaven is filled with those who have this in common:
They are forgiven. And they forgive."*
—President Dieter F. Uchtdorf

FORGIVING SOMEONE, ESPECIALLY YOUR SPOUSE, is a Christlike attribute necessary for a happy marriage. Satan encourages the opposite—he rejoices when we refuse to forgive. He does not want us to be forgiving; he can whisper convincing justifications for our harboring ill will. Such behavior allows him to drive destructive wedges into our marriage.

We all make mistakes that need our spouse's forgiveness. Some mistakes are small and insignificant, while others are serious with eternal consequences. All need to be dealt with. Amends need to be made. President Gordon B. Hinckley said,

> In our day the Lord has said in revelation: "Wherefore, I say unto you, that ye ought to forgive one another; for he that forgiveth not his brother his trespasses standeth condemned before the Lord; for there remaineth in him the greater sin.
>
> "I, the Lord, will forgive whom I will forgive, but of you it is required to forgive all men" (D&C 64:9–10). The Lord has offered a marvelous promise. Said He, "He who has repented of his sins, the same is forgiven, and I, the Lord, remember them no more" (D&C 58:42).

President Hinckley continued with this sad lament:

> There are so many in our day who are unwilling
> to forgive and forget. Children cry and wives weep
> because fathers and husbands continue to bring up
> little shortcomings that are really of no importance.
> And there also are many women who would make a
> mountain out of every little offending molehill of word
> or deed.[1]

Offenses come in degrees. They usually fall into three categories of
seriousness. The first, the minor ones, we'll call Molehill-size Offenses.
The second, a bit more serious and in need of attention, we'll call
Foothill-size Offenses. The last, which are of major importance, we'll
call Mountain-size Offenses.

MOLEHILL-SIZE OFFENSES

President Hinckley makes a good point. Too much is too often made of
minor offenses. Let's first consider offenses that may fall into the category
of "little shortcomings" and "molehills" in marriage relationships. We'll
lump them both under the heading of Molehill-size Offenses. We'll
address only a few of them here.

Molehill-size Offense #1: Forgot a Birthday or Anniversary
In our busy lives, this sometimes happens. It is far from tragic, but it
can be hurtful. We all like to be remembered on our special day. If you
are the one who forgot, apologize and do something to make up for it.
The card racks are filled with belated birthday cards. You might even
find one that says outright, "Forgive me for forgetting your birthday."
If not, make your own, then make a date and go celebrate. "Better late
than never" is a sentiment that works in this case. If you are the one
whose birthday was forgotten, let your spouse know in a loving way
and suggest what you could do to celebrate, even if it's later. Then both
of you go have some fun and don't hold a grudge. It's not worth it.

If it's a wedding anniversary that's coming up, remember it's a day
that belongs to both of you, so plan ahead—together. Don't wait for the
other to do all the planning and then blame him or her for forgetting it.
Help each other remember these days and there will be no forgetting or

hurt feelings—and thus no need for forgiveness. Help each other find ways to celebrate special occasions. Marriage is not a "gotcha" game where you are looking for ways your mate has let you down.

Molehill-size Offense #2: Gave an Angry Response Spoken in the Heat of the Moment

No one wants to be treated unkindly, especially by a spouse. Maybe you were upset by something your spouse did—for example, maybe your wife accidently backed into a pole in a parking lot and put a dent in the bumper of your new car. Out of frustration, when you found out, you snapped at her with a comment like, "How the heck did you let that happen?"

Remember the only person who feels worse than you about this is your wife. Cut her some slack and treat her with respect. Accidents happen. If you are the wife and your husband has just snapped at you, you can choose to do one of the following three things.

- You can snap back with equal unkindness and be mad at him for not understanding. After all, he wasn't there with a bunch of kids causing major distractions in the car. You're mad at him for his lack of compassion. In your mind you're thinking of a way to get even, and you can hardly wait until he makes a mistake so you can rub his nose in it.
- You can ignore his remark and let it fester inside. Things not discussed can grow out of proportion, and then suddenly you explode and let him have a volley of verbal abuse—a taste of his own medicine.
- Or you can put yourself in his shoes for a minute and validate his frustration. Watch what happens when you say, "I don't blame you for being upset. I am, too. It's our new car and I'm sick about it." Watch how that calms him down. When you put yourself in someone else's shoes emotionally, it's the first step to forgiving an offense.

If you're the one who made the original unkind remark, recognize your error and apologize. You may say something like, "I'm sorry, honey. I know you didn't mean for it to happen. Please forgive me." It has been said that an apology is the super glue of life that can repair just about anything.

Molehill-size Offense #3: Insulted Your Cooking

Maybe he was just being honest. He may not have liked what you served. It's true he needs to find a kinder way of saying he didn't like it, or he may need to learn to just be quiet about it and be grateful you fixed a meal for him and your family. If your mate asks you if you like what she cooked, and you didn't like it, you could respond with a comment like, "I appreciate your fixing dinner. However, I'd be okay if you didn't fix this one again." Or "Thanks, honey, but this one isn't one of my favorites like so many others you cook." A kind response is the key. Then forget about it. Both of you.

Molehill-size Offense #4: Won't Hang Up His Clothes

You've told your mate you would like a clean, neat home, and still he leaves his clothes slung over the chair. One woman, early in her marriage, became so exasperated over it she almost nailed her husband's coat to the floor where he continually dropped it after work. She finally decided that would not be a good idea.

One day she was thinking about all the wonderful traits her husband had and decided him dropping his clothes all over was no big deal. From that day on she ignored the clothes, picked them up when they bothered her, and didn't nag him about it again. That may not be the answer for someone else, but it worked for her. She simply forgave him of this indiscretion and moved on, appreciating the good in him. He came to appreciate his wife and her ability to overlook certain annoying habits, some of which he overcame. Still some persisted, even when he later served as bishop and then stake president. She realized too that there were many things she did that surely must annoy him but that he had overlooked. They lived a life of forgiving the molehills, which allowed their marriage to flourish.

FOOTHILL-SIZE OFFENSES

These offenses are not as easily dismissed as the molehill-size kind. They hurt more deeply and need to be resolved, though they are not marriage-threatening in nature. We'll call these the Foothill-size Offenses. Here are a few that fit into this category.

Foothill-size Offense #1: Says Rude Things about Your Parents
Imagine your spouse says something like, "Your mother is a nosy busy-body and needs to stay out of our business!" That could hurt. Before reacting to the unwelcome comment, think for a minute and ask yourself if there is merit in what your spouse is saying. Something is driving this kind of comment. Have a calm conversation and discuss what it is. It may be that some boundaries need to be set with your parents.

Learning to get along with in-laws is part of every marriage. Talk calmly with each other and come to an agreement about what should and should not be said about each other's parents. Then forgive hurtful things that were said before you had this talk. And don't bring it up again. If it happens again, bite your tongue and resist the temptation to say, "There you go again!" Just calmly have that "talk" again. If your parents are meddling, it may mean you need to have the talk with them—time to set those boundaries. Let them know you love them, and kindly tell them to stop interfering in your marriage. Don't let this foothill grow into a mountain between you and your spouse.

Foothill-size Offense #2: Doesn't Appreciate How Hard You Work
You work hard to provide for your family. At times you think your wife does not understand the difficulties you face on the job and how you keep on working in order to keep a roof overhead.

She may even compare you to a friend's spouse who makes more money, and say, "Why can't you get a better job, like Jim?" This can hurt deeply. You can respond with equal fervor and say, "Hey, I work my head off for you and the kids. Too bad you didn't marry Jim instead of me!"

With these responses both of you have jumped into the trap Satan has set. If your wife actually said that, or something like it, here's a response you might try: "I know it's hard to make the money stretch to meet all our needs. I wish I were making more. I really appreciate how good you are at making it all work. I'm lucky I married you."

Or if you think it's a possibility, you might add, "I'm keeping my eyes open for a better job. Let's pray tonight that we will be guided to have the money we need to live on." She will likely soften and be more grateful for your efforts. Then your job is to forgive her angry comment and do your best to show her love and gratitude.

What about the wife whose husband does not appreciate all she does to keep their home functioning and their children cared for? That can be equally hurtful with comments such as, "I hate coming home to a messy house. Why can't you keep our home clean like my sister keeps hers?" Never compare your wife to another woman. Most husbands have no idea of the many challenges that arise in a day that thwart his wife's homemaking goals. Give your wife the benefit of the doubt. Instead, notice what did get done and compliment her on it. If you see something that needs doing, jump in and offer your help.

If your husband said something that hurt your feelings regarding your efforts at home, you could hold the caustic comeback and instead say, "I know it's disappointing to come home to a mess. Could we sit down for a minute and you let me tell you about my day? If you have some good suggestions after hearing me out, I would be happy to consider them." Communication is the key to understanding each other's daily challenges.

Foothill-size Offense #3: Discounted My Tears
Sometimes a wife can experience a sadness that can't help but bring tears—even sobbing, if it's a genuine sorrow in her life. A response such as, "You need to get over it," will only prolong the sorrow. A spouse must not discount those tears. Her heart is aching. She may have been betrayed by a good friend or lost a job she enjoyed. These are huge things in a person's life. If you think she should stop crying and move on, you are being insensitive to her needs.

Tears are normal and even necessary in the process of healing from sorrow. Showing compassion and understanding will keep it from becoming a mountain. If you have discounted your spouse's sorrow, it's time to back up and ask for forgiveness. Then give a good measure of tender loving care. Your turn will come, and she will know how to return the favor because of the love and kindness you showed to her. If you were the offended one, you need to accept his apology and forgive him without bringing it up again.

We can hold grudges in hundreds of ways and let offenses get out of hand. The best thing to do is to ignore what doesn't matter and pay attention to those that do. If these offenses have occurred in your marriage, apologize, be forgiving, and move on to the things that really matter. Greater love and harmony will grow in your home.

Elder Robert L. Simpson counseled, "Every couple, whether in the first or the twenty-first year of marriage, should discover the value of pillow-talk time at the end of the day—the perfect time to take inventory, to talk about tomorrow. And best of all, it's a time when love and appreciation for one another can be reconfirmed. The end of another day is also the perfect setting to say, 'Sweetheart, I am sorry about what happened today. Please forgive me.'"2

MOUNTAIN-SIZE OFFENSES
Some offenses are so serious in nature that hearts are broken—as well as covenants—and all trust is lost. We'll discuss a few of the most prominent ones. These are the Mountain-size Offenses that have broken too many marriages.

Mountain-size Offense #1: Spouse Had Sexual Relations with Someone Else
When your covenanted companion has an affair, finding out is like being stabbed in the heart with a dagger. The pain is real and deep. It feels like you've been run over by a truck and left broken and bleeding on the side of the road, and no one has the ability to pick you up and make you all better. You feel completely alone and forsaken in your pain.

Let's suppose this happened to you—and let's suppose that your mate recognized how terribly wrong it was and regrets it to the depth of her soul. She begs to be forgiven and is on the road to repentance. Can you forgive her, if it's your wife? Can you forgive him, if it's your husband?

Elder Dallin H. Oaks explained that, "Under the law of the Lord, a marriage, like a human life, is a precious, living thing. If our bodies are sick, we seek to heal them. We do not give up. While there is any prospect of life, we seek healing again and again. The same should be true of our marriages, and if we seek Him, the Lord will help us and heal us."3 That goes for both the offender and the offended. Both need healing. That's what accessing the Atonement is all about.

Maggie and Jeff understood this principle. In their case, Jeff was the offender. He had had multiple affairs during an eight-year period. Maggie knew nothing of it, since he was gone a lot in his line of work. She also had no way of knowing because he expressed love to her and their six children and kept on fulfilling his Church callings. She was completely in the dark regarding his secret life of adultery. She found out when the guilt eventually overwhelmed him. He finally broke down and confessed his sins to his bishop, who told him to go home and confess them to his wife. She had to know.

Maggie was devastated. She described that experience as a feeling of all her breath being taken away. She literally fell to the floor in agony. It was almost more than she could bear. How could he do this to her and their family? How could he have done it for so long and she not know? How could he ever be forgiven by the Lord for such a heavy sin? How could she forgive him? What was to happen to their marriage? All of these questions and many more swirled around in her head.

Jeff continually begged for her forgiveness. He felt terrible to have caused the kind of agony his wife was experiencing. However, such transgression is not the sort of thing that goes away because your mate apologizes and is remorseful and is on his road of repentance. No. This type of offense takes a long time to heal. President Boyd K. Packer taught, "To earn forgiveness, one must make restitution. That means you give back what you have taken or ease the pain of those you have injured."[4] Jeff worked daily at easing Maggie's pain.

Because he was in a priesthood leadership position, the law of justice had to be met; he was excommunicated, thus losing all his temple and priesthood blessings. His agony was also deeply painful.

Jeff begged Maggie to not leave him. After much prayer and millions of tears, Maggie decided to stay in the marriage. However, at one point, she realized if she were to do her part in saving their marriage, she had to exercise mercy. Elder Jeffrey R. Holland reminds us, "When it comes to our own sins, we don't ask for justice. What we plead for is mercy—and that is what we must be willing to give."[5]

Through long months of prayerful pleading for understanding and patience, Maggie was finally able to give mercy to her husband. She was then able to forgive him. Step by step she felt the blessings of the Atonement pour down upon her. She was not alone, after all.

Christ was there to bear her burden and lift her sorrow. She accepted His gift. And so did Jeff. It was only through accepting the gift of the Atonement that he finally felt forgiven by the Lord. He patiently waited the required number of years and was rebaptized. His temple and priesthood blessings were restored a couple of years later. It was worth the wait.

Maggie and Jeff fought the bitter battle and came out victorious. They then began to do what all couples must do, which is to be completely devoted and loving to each other. They prayed together, they played together, and they attended the temple together again and again. They rebuilt their marriage, and now, after many years, are happy together enjoying their grandchildren and serving missions for the Lord. They found the joy of true repentance and forgiveness.

President Thomas S. Monson encourages those who may be in this same situation. He reminds us of what the Lord said to those who repent: "Though your sins be as scarlet, they shall be as white as snow. . . . And I will remember them no more."[6]

Mountain-size Offense #2: Spouse Is Involved in Pornography

If your spouse is involved in pornography, he or she needs your love and help more than ever. Don't let disgust and repulsion for the act consume the love you have for your mate. Those are Satan's tools. In the chapter on Safeguard #8, "Stay Away from Pornography," you will discover how treacherous this sin can be and how devastating it is on a marriage. We learn from Elder Dallin H. Oaks's comments that levels of pornographic involvement exist.[7] You will also find that the sooner the problem is dealt with, the easier it is to overcome. Even the hardest case, defined as addiction, can be healed through the Atonement of Christ.

We recently heard of a couple where the husband, who had been deeply involved and addicted to pornography, had worked hard to overcome the problem. There were slipups along the way, but with the help of professional counseling and a caring bishop, he is now free of this terrible addiction. Here's the catch. Even though it has been well more than a year, his wife can't seem to forget what he did; she brings it up over and over. She even has told her friends about it. This is not how forgiveness works. In order for him to be completely healed, she needs to truly forgive him and put it far back in her mind until it is finally forgotten. By bringing it up to him and others, she makes it impossible for herself and him to forget.

Sadly, she continually brings up how awful he was during the time he was addicted to porn. No matter how many times he apologizes, she will not let it go. It's a terrible strain on their marriage. What could be a happy result of a changed soul lingers in the air like a black cloud. One can only hope that she will finally accept the Atonement and completely forgive her husband.

We'll not dwell further on this subject since it's well covered in the chapter dealing with pornography, except to say this: When a spouse has repented of this offense, do not bring it up again. Never throw it in the face of your spouse if you happen to be mad about something else. That's like fueling a fire you have worked so hard to put out.

To forgive and forget is vital to permanent healing of this offense. Elder Dale G. Renlund reminds us, "As we change, we will find that God indeed cares a lot more about who we are and about who we are becoming than about who we once were."[8] That's the kind of caring we need to have for each other as husbands and wives.

Mountain-size Offense #3: Spouse Is Addicted to Pain Medication
Any drug addiction is a serious problem that must be dealt with. Because addiction to pain medication is a serious problem for far too many Latter-day Saints, this is our focus here. People need to know that it is plain and simply a type of drug abuse that, if not corrected, can cause death. The Centers for Disease Control and Prevention reported that 47,055 people in the United States died from a drug overdose in 2014—more than any other year on record. Some 61 percent of those fatal overdoses involved heroin and opioids, mostly prescription painkillers like OxyContin or Percocet. These deaths were characterized as "prescription" opioid overdoses.[9]

In addition to the risk of death, this addiction causes change in personalities, which can seriously affect marriage relationships. People who are addicted to these types of drugs often become withdrawn, angry, or even may be abusive and out of control, particularly if they are denied their drugs. It may not seem like a sin, such as taking street drugs, but it can become every bit as harmful. Just because it begins with a prescription from a physician doesn't mean its continued misuse is justified.

In her article "Prescription Drugs: The Hidden Addiction," author Darla Isackson said,

> Most [people] addicted to prescription drugs would never consider using alcohol or illicit drugs. Prescription drugs, however, are legitimate, sanctioned, even encouraged for many problems, yet can easily lead to a dependence not intended or invited. Once [someone] is innocently ensnared, guilt coupled with the feared stigma of judgment or disapproval can create barriers to treatment and increased reason for denial.[10]

Elder M. Russell Ballard clarified the proper use of prescription drugs when he said,

> Now, brothers and sisters, please don't misunderstand what I am saying. I'm not questioning prescription medications for those suffering with treatable illness or great physical pain. They are indeed a blessing. What I am saying is that we need to carefully follow the doses prescribed by doctors. And we need to keep such medications in a safe place where youngsters or anyone else cannot gain access to them.[11]

When prescribed doses have been ignored and abused, that's when problems begin. To those caught in this trap, life can seem hopeless. Elder Ballard went on to say,

> But no matter what addictive cycle one is caught in, there is always hope. The prophet Lehi taught his sons this eternal truth: "Wherefore, men are free according to the flesh; and all things are given them which are expedient unto man. And they are free to choose liberty and eternal life, through the great Mediator of all men, or to choose captivity and death, according to the captivity and power of the devil" (2 Nephi 2:27).[12]

Elder Ballard continued by suggesting help to overcome such an addiction. For more information, read his entire talk, "O That Cunning Plan of the Evil One," in the November 2010 issue of the *Ensign*.

In this chapter we are dealing with the principle of forgiveness. Without delving further into the effects and treatments for this type of drug addiction, we'll move into a couple of cases of real people dealing with this issue and how forgiveness fits into the picture as it relates to marriage.

Simon and Lisa faced this difficulty. After a serious accident, Lisa suffered severe pain. Her doctor prescribed medication to get her through the worst time. When the need was no longer there, she felt she still needed the medication to get through the day. She was hooked. Her behavior changed, and she became somewhat abusive to her husband—yelling at him, being impatient, and being unkind. Simon felt betrayed by her lack of concern for him during this time. She would not listen to his counsel concerning the problem. Nor would she go for professional help.

After two years he began to fear for his wife's life and insisted she enter a drug rehabilitation center. It wasn't easy at first, but then the treatment began to bear fruit. She had been a faithful Church member and was reminded by her bishop of the power of the Atonement in helping her recover. Through the help of this drug addiction program, her husband, her bishop, her parents, other caring individuals, and mighty prayers (both hers and Simon's), Lisa was finally cured.

Lisa believed the words of Elder Richard G. Scott: "The fruit of true repentance is forgiveness, which opens the door to receive all the covenants and ordinances provided on this earth and to enjoy the resulting blessings."[13] Lisa had been angry with Simon for insisting on the treatment, and he had been upset at her for resisting for so long. Both of them had to forgive each other and appreciate their new life.

These words of Elder Scott hold the answer: "When memory of past mistakes encroaches upon your mind, turn your thoughts to the Redeemer and to the miracle of forgiveness with the renewal that comes through Him. Your depression and suffering will be replaced by peace, joy, and gratitude for His love."[14]

In another case, as seen on the BYU TV show *Story Trek*, we learned of a wife who was able to forgive years of her husband's pain medication addiction. She said she spent those years "walking on eggshells" so as not to enrage him. She never knew what he might do at any moment if she said the wrong thing that could set him off. Still she hung on, cherishing her marriage and hoping for a change.

She testified that through the power of God's help, her husband was finally healed. She has found peace in forgiving him and enjoying the man he was before the drugs entered his life. They are now happily married, rejoicing in the results of repentance and forgiveness.

Her actions bear out these words of Elder Jeffrey R. Holland: "Broken minds can be healed just the way broken bones and broken hearts are healed. While God is at work making those repairs, the rest of us can help by being merciful, nonjudgmental, and kind."[15]

Mountain-size Offense #4: Spouse Is Arrested and Sent to Prison
Never in a million years would you think your beloved spouse would end up in prison. But what if it happens? Someone experiencing this tragedy said, "It feels like a nightmare and you just want to wake up and have it be over. But instead, it's real." That's when "married for better or worse" takes on new meaning. Now the question comes: can you forgive your spouse for doing this to you and our family? The answer to that needs to be yes. However, the other question is, would you be willing to stay married to your imprisoned mate? The seriousness of the crime has everything to do with the answer. If the crime is one that can be forgiven by the Lord, it can be forgiven by you. Only fervent prayer and counseling with your bishop can lead you to know what you need to do.

Here is an actual case where the wife had to decide if she would stay married to her incarcerated husband. Daniel and Wendy (not their real names) had a temple marriage and two grown children. They loved each other and never dreamed this tragedy would be part of their lives. Daniel got caught up in a business venture that led to fraud. He was not the instigator, but he knew about it and did not report it. That's all it took for a jury to convict him, right along with the others involved.

Daniel was sorry beyond words for not doing the right thing. He did not deny his guilt and knew punishment had to be part of his repentance. He sincerely apologized to Wendy for the pain he caused her and his family. Wendy was heartsick. She had no knowledge of what had been going on. She loved Daniel and knew she would stick with him through this nightmare he and she faced. Seven years in prison is a long time. The thing that made her willing to stay was the fact that he was doing everything in his power to repent and make things right. She visited him regularly. Wendy's comfortable lifestyle changed dramatically, and she had to find a job to make ends meet. She also had to move out of their lovely home into a small apartment.

Wendy understood that though this time was difficult, it was a temporary bump on the road to their eternal marriage. Through prayer, fasting, and temple attendance, she found the strength to hold on. Finally Daniel was released from prison. She now had a choice. She could forgive him enough to never say anything that would make him feel worse than he already felt, or she could keep bringing it up. She chose to let it go and do all she could to help her husband adjust and become the man she knew he really was. She truly forgave him, and they were able to move forward toward their eternal goals.

Elder Dallin H. Oaks gave wise counsel for all couples facing these kinds of challenges. He said, "Don't treasure up past wrongs, reprocessing them again and again. In a marriage relationship, festering is destructive; forgiving is divine (see D&C 64:9–10). Plead for the guidance of the Spirit of the Lord to forgive wrongs . . . to overcome faults, and to strengthen relationships."[16] Every case is different and must be faced with faith and a determination to seek the Lord's will, then follow it.

CONCLUSION

Many offenses exist that we have not addressed, but the principles apply to all. We know that forgiveness is vital if a marriage relationship is to endure. President Gordon B. Hinckley said, "A spirit of forgiveness and an attitude of love and compassion toward those who may have wronged us is of the very essence of the gospel of Jesus Christ. Each of us has need of this spirit. The whole world has need of it. The Lord taught it. He exemplified it as none other has exemplified it."[17]

Ideally, when we forgive we eventually forget. Some offenses may have been so hurtful that, even after all is forgiven, it's difficult to completely forget. We suggest you do your best to set those aside, and eventually they will no longer find a place in your thoughts.

We conclude with the words of Elder Lynn G. Robbins from his book, *Love Is a Choice*. He wrote, "[E]very couple will encounter some struggles on their journey toward this glorious destiny. A happy and successful marriage depends on two people who are good at forgiving, or as President Gordon B. Hinckley pointed out, have learned 'a high degree of mutual toleration.' True and mature love is manifest after we discover each other's imperfections and still commit to one another."[18]

Notes

1. Gordon B. Hinckley, "Forgiveness," *Ensign*, Nov. 2005.

2. Robert L. Simpson, "A Lasting Marriage," *Ensign*, May 1982.

3. Dallin H. Oaks, "Divorce," *Ensign*, May 2007.

4. Boyd K. Packer, "The Brilliant Morning of Forgiveness," *Ensign*, Nov. 1995.

5. Jeffrey R. Holland, "Amazed at the Love Jesus Offers Me," *Liahona*, Dec. 2008.

6. Thomas S. Monson, "Keep the Commandments," *Ensign*, Nov. 2015.

7. See Dallin H. Oaks, "Recovering from the Trap of Pornography," *Ensign*, Oct. 2015.

8. Dale G. Renlund, "Latter-day Saints Keep on Trying," *Ensign*, May 2015.

9. See Rose A. Rudd, Noah Aleshire, Jon E. Zibbell, and R. Matthew Gladden, "Increases in Drug and Opioid Overdose Deaths—United States, 2000–2014," *Centers for Disease Control and Prevention*, Jan. 1, 2016, http://www.cdc.gov/mmwr/preview/mmwrhtml/mm6450a3.htm.

10. Darla Isackson, "Prescription Drugs: The Hidden Addiction," *Meridian Magazine*, Jul. 12, 2013, http://ldsmag.com/article-1-12970/.

11. M. Russell Ballard, "O That Cunning Plan of the Evil One," *Ensign*, Nov. 2010.

12. Ibid.

13. Richard G. Scott, "Finding Forgiveness," *Ensign*, May 1995.

14. Richard G. Scott, "The Path to Peace and Joy," *Ensign*, Nov. 2000.

15. Jeffrey R. Holland, "Like a Broken Vessel," *Ensign*, Nov. 2013.

16. Dallin H. Oaks, "Divorce," *Ensign*, May 2007.

17. Gordon B. Hinckley, "Of You It Is Required to Forgive," *Ensign*, Jun. 1991.

18. Lynn G. Robbins, "Elder Robbins: How to Build a Love That Lasts Forever," *LDS Living*, http://www.ldsliving.com/Elder-Robbins-How-to-Build-a-Love-That-Lasts-Forever/s/81055?utm_source=ldsliving&utm_medium=email.

SAFEGUARD #12
Be Wise in Your Spending

*"All too often a family's spending is governed more by their
yearning than by their earning."*
—Elder Joseph B. Wirthlin

WISELY MANAGING YOUR FAMILY INCOME is a vitally important way you can safeguard your marriage. A Kansas State University researcher found that "Arguments about money [are] by far the top predictor of divorce. It's not children, sex, in-laws or anything else. It's money—for both men and women."[1] Satan is well aware of this trap and will use everything in his bag of tricks to tempt you to misuse your money. The temptations can be great in a world that glorifies material possessions.

When financial woes escalate and couples blame each other, the idea of divorce can feel like the best solution. If anyone thinks divorce will stop money problems, think again. Divorce magnifies the problem in greater ways that are unimaginable for both parties.

Knowing this, couples need to do everything in their power to be united in solving financial challenges. Family money is sacred. It's not for one spouse to selfishly spend without discussing purchases with the other. That's why sitting down and making a financial plan together is so important. Goals are identified and worked toward together. It takes both husband and wife to make the plan succeed.

BUYING A HOME
In their desire to have a beautiful home, couples sometimes jointly make decisions they later regret. The adversary is expert at putting

thoughts into their minds that they need to have a lovely home like Joe
and Jane. After all, they believe they deserve it as much as anyone else.
Coveting what others have never works.

To make a wise purchase on something as big as a home, important
questions need to be considered.

1. What do we really need?
2. What can we honestly afford?
3. What do we want that is within our budget?
4. Can we afford the taxes on it?
5. Can we afford the insurance and the upkeep?
6. What is our backup plan if the economy fails?
7. What if we suffer a job loss?

A few years ago when the economy took a plunge and the housing
market crashed, many people who had purchased beautiful new homes
without first considering the above questions ended up in serious
trouble. Many of them lost everything. Their financial planning had
not included "what-if" possibilities. Many ended up with up-side-
down loans—their mortgage was higher than their house was now
worth. Many lost everything because they bought too much for their
ability to pay in case of a downturn in the economy.

President Gordon B. Hinckley gave wise counsel when he said, "I
recognize that it may be necessary to borrow to get a home, of course.
But let us buy a home that we can afford and thus ease the payments
which will constantly hang over our heads without mercy or respite for
as long as 30 years. No one knows when emergencies will strike."[2]

Church leaders have counseled couples to not only buy wisely, but
to pay off their homes as soon as possible. In the biography of his life,
I Will Lead You Along, President Henry B. Eyring told of his dilemma
regarding home buying. In 1973, while he was president of Ricks
College (now BYU–Idaho) in Rexburg, Idaho, through wise planning
he and his wife were able to make a substantial down payment on
a new home there. Still, a sizable debt remained. Fortunately, again
through wise planning and hard work, their home was their only debt.

During that time he heard a general conference talk by Elder Ezra
Taft Benson,[3] in which Elder Benson quoted President J. Reuben
Clark, Jr. of the First Presidency, from a talk given in 1937. President
Clark said, "Let us avoid debt as we would avoid a plague; where we are

now in debt, let us get out of debt; if not today, then tomorrow. Let us straitly and strictly live within our incomes, and save a little."
President Eyring said,

> After quoting President Clark, Elder Benson added his personal promise: "For the righteous the gospel provides a warning before a calamity, a program for the crises, a refuge for each disaster." He also added an admonition: "The Lord desires his saints to be free and independent in the critical days ahead. But no man is truly free who is in financial bondage."[4]

Doing all he could to pay off the debt on his house, President Eyring said that a purely rational investment adviser would have told him to make only the minimum required payment against the mortgage and put any free cash into commodities such as gold or oil, where he stood to make a bundle.[5]

He immediately sold some holdings he and his wife had, which by some miracle (these happen when we follow the counsel of the prophets) were now available. With this they were able to pay off their home mortgage. He came to know there is power in listening to and obeying our Church leaders.

President Hinckley told of a similar example:

> President Faust would not tell you this himself. Perhaps I can tell it, and he can take it out on me afterward. He had a mortgage on his home drawing 4 percent interest. Many people would have told him he was foolish to pay off that mortgage when it carried so low a rate of interest. But the first opportunity he had to acquire some means, he and his wife determined they would pay off their mortgage. He has been free of debt since that day. That's why he wears a smile on his face, and that's why he whistles while he works.[6]

Every couple can find a way to pay off a home mortgage in a relative short time by applying a few extra dollars to the principle payment each month. They can also limit other expenditures and apply that amount to the principle. It's impressive how soon a mortgage is paid off when these practices are applied.

BUYING A CAR

Cars can also be a temptation to couples. It's fun to have a nice new car—until the payments come bearing down on you during a hard time. We personally learned long ago, after a few unwise new-car purchases, that buying a one- or two-year-old car is much wiser. Letting the first-time buyer pay the price of that first year of depreciation is like money in the bank. Many cars previously owned by car rental companies, who replace their cars yearly, end up being an excellent buy. And here's the bonus: the warranty is still in place. People save thousands of dollars by purchasing a car in this way. Do your best to save up and pay cash. That way you lose no money on interest.

Even so, be sure to keep within your budget. Don't let greed take over wisdom. Be sure you can afford what you buy. Remember, when you buy a car you also buy ongoing insurance and occasional repairs. You must be able to afford the car and the expenses that come with it.

PLAN TOGETHER

Sometimes a mate has such a strong desire to buy something that he or she buys it without telling his or her spouse. Such was the case with Nancy and Jerry.

> Nancy found it difficult to manage a budget when her husband would make purchasing decisions without consulting her. He wanted to landscape their yard, for example, and a friend convinced him to purchase railroad ties, dozens of plants, and create a beautiful three-tiered backyard. He never gave Nancy the opportunity to tell him they couldn't afford it.
>
> Jerry couldn't understand why Nancy was so upset by his behavior. He thought she was a nag. "I didn't see I was making any mistakes," he recalls. "I thought she had a real problem with anger."
>
> [Later] they would lie in bed at night thinking, "How did I get myself into this mess? How can I get out of this thing?"[7]

Fortunately Nancy and Jerry wanted to make their marriage work. They turned to God and others to help find a solution to their financial problems. They created a plan that worked for both of them and together overcame the problem.

In an effective financial plan, there needs to be room in a budget for a certain amount of unaccounted-for spending needs to be available to both husband and wife. Buying a tube of lipstick or a hamburger should not need the permission of a spouse. Decide how much you are willing for each to have to spend however you wish, then stick to it. Some have set $50 a month as the limit. Some set a limit of less, and some more. The amount is up the couple and their income. If you want to buy something costing more than that, then have the discussion, and purchase only what the two of you agree upon, according to what you can honestly afford.

THE CREDIT CARD TRAP

One of the most devastating culprits in the misuse of money is credit cards. These make instant gratification so easy. "Buy now and repent later" too easily becomes the destructive motto of many. Credit card spending that spirals out of control can ruin a marriage. If both partners are reckless in using charge cards, it's double trouble. The day of reckoning will come, and it will not be a pretty picture.

Maybe just one of you is the culprit. If your wife happens to be the one who charged enough to compete with the national debt (well, maybe not quite), here's what you can do. First, don't blow your top. It may seem like the end of the world when a debt pit is so deep it feels like there is no way to climb out of it. A way is always open if the charging and spending stop and a plan of action is begun. Here's what to do.

Calmly have a serious talk about the gravity of the situation. Let her explain what she was doing. Sometimes women charge to buy their little ones designer clothes, the latest toys, or to buy expensive clothes, jewelry, or spa visits for themselves. The list goes on. Men also find it tempting to indulge their wants on electronic devices, tools, new golf clubs, or any number of items that catch their interest. Whatever either spends that violates the budget proves that together you need to make a plan to create financial security. Be understanding, patient, and kind as you work together to solve the problem.

It's true, it takes a lot of money to raise kids; however, they can get along on a lot less than you may think. Spoiling them doesn't prepare them for life as much as helping them earn their own way will. If your spouse is willing to look at the situation and apologize for reckless spending on the kids and other items, accept the apology. If one (or both) of you does not have the discipline to use credit cards by paying the full balance each month without borrowing from your savings to do it, then your days of using credit cards needs to be over. It's time to do the following.

- Shred all of your credit cards and pay cash for what you buy.

- Put all things other than actual necessities on hold as you pay down the credit card balance.

- If more than one credit card was used, pay down the smallest balance first while paying the minimum payment on the others. When that balance is zero, take that amount and apply it to the next smallest balance. When that one is paid, take the amount you would have been paying on both of the paid-off ones and apply the amount to the next one. If you have any extra funds, apply them to that balance. Before you know it you will have them all paid off. Financial expert Dave Ramsey calls this the "Snowball Method." Just as a snowball gathers more snow as it rolls down a hill, so does money applied to the next payment gain more money. The key is to avoid adding any more debt along the way. Any extra money goes to paying off the next debt balance.

- Make a plan for spending based on what your income allows. Don't waver. Stick to the plan. That is the only way to get ahead.

Elder Joseph B. Wirthlin said, "Remember this: debt is a form of bondage. It is a financial termite. When we make purchases on credit, they give us only an illusion of prosperity. We think we own things, but the reality is, our things own us."[8]

For more information on how to get out of debt, consider following the debt-free plan of financial guru Dave Ramsey at DaveRamsey.com, or find your own financial planner with a proven record. Counsel with your bishop. He may know the perfect person to help you learn how to manage your money. Be willing to learn. Part of repenting of over-spending is making a sensible change.

Start walking this path together without bringing up past indiscretions. Go forward with determination and forgiveness, and it's amazing what you can accomplish.

EVILS OF GAMBLING

Before we leave the debt problem, we must acknowledge that buying things is not the only devil in the game. Gambling has ruined many marriages. We have seen people lose their home, their marriage, and everything they have over gambling. It can take over your life like an addictive drug and reel you in. If either of you has a serious gambling problem, it's urgent that you see a counselor and get help immediately.

According to an online divorce site,

> The money issue that no one wants to talk about is family income spent on gambling. This is a far bigger problem than most people think. Many people who are married to a gambler pull the plug on the marriage because they see it as the only way to prevent eventual financial ruin. The sad part in these cases is that frequently the marriage is "good" apart from one spouse's gambling addiction.[9]

Several years ago we bought some property for investment purposes. It was a great deal for us. As we later found out, the man selling the property had to sell this choice piece of land to cover a gambling debt. He not only lost his property, but he lost his marriage. We were sad for the man who lost so much because of this terrible addiction.

Gambling can start small and seem insignificant. A quarter in the slot machine, a simple lottery ticket, betting on a sports game, laying down a little cash on a horse race, and on it goes. They are all gambling. The Church has made clear its stand regarding gambling.

Elder Dallin H. Oaks said, "There can be no question about the moral ramifications of gambling. As it has in the past, The Church of Jesus Christ of Latter-day Saints stands opposed to gambling, including government-sponsored lotteries."[10]

President Gordon B. Hinckley said,

> Gambling is to be found almost everywhere and is growing. People play poker. They bet on horse races

and dog races. They play roulette and work the slot machines. They gather to play in bars, saloons, and casinos, and, all too often, in their own homes. Many cannot leave it alone. It becomes addictive. In so many cases it leads to other destructive habits and practices.

And so very many of those who become involved cannot afford the money it takes. In many cases it robs wives and children of financial security.[11]

The following case, where names are changed to protect privacy, bears this out. Kris, whose husband, Sheldon, is addicted to gambling, knows only too well the devastation gambling can bring. She has begged him to stop. The debt from his gambling losses keeps mounting. Still he keeps on, always with the illusive hope that he will win big and all will be well. Satan is clever in his ability to keep someone hooked. He makes sure a few small wins happen occasionally to keep the hope alive. And yet, the debt keeps climbing. Kris said Sheldon is so obsessed with it that he secretly slips away to Las Vegas and racks up more and more debt.

His high-paying job as a business consultant is now in jeopardy. His career is about to be ruined. Kris fears they are about to lose their home. Credit card companies are hounding them for payments beyond what they can meet. Nearly all expenditures tie back to gambling and the money it takes for his gambling trips.

Kris keeps praying that Sheldon will awaken and change his ways. She prays, fasts, attends the temple, and seeks counsel from her bishop and from a professional counselor. She is doing all in her power to save her marriage. Sometimes their only child, now a mother herself, and other family members who are aware of the problem tell her to leave him, thinking that may be what it takes to wake him up. Kris does not believe that is the answer. She still loves Sheldon and wants to save their marriage.

Sheldon's problem is a heavy load, but recently Kris felt a glimmer of hope. No one knows the outcome of her situation yet, but this much she knows: God is comforting her and blessing her with greater peace in recent days than she has experienced for years. She is beginning to see a light at the end of this very dark tunnel. Even though it is small, she sees an awakening happening in Sheldon. She knows the power of the Atonement and how it can bless her and her husband. This knowledge helps her hold on.

President Dieter F. Uchtdorf's counsel seems to fit situations such as this. He said,

> The more we obsess about our difficulties, our struggles, our doubts, and our fears, the more difficult things can become. But the more we focus on our final heavenly destination and on the joys of following the disciple's path—loving God, serving our neighbor— the more likely we are to successfully navigate through times of trouble and turbulence.[12]

We urge you to never get caught in the trap of gambling. If you never do it once, you will never do it a second time.

A GET-OUT-OF-DEBT PLAN

It's possible to get out of debt even on a meager income. Here's how one couple with two children did it while living on their $36,000 a year income. They said, "When you only have $200 to spend on groceries, you have to really analyze your choices and buy only the things that are going to be of nutritional benefit."[13] Here's what they did:

- Eliminated junk food, such as packaged cookies, candy, chips, and sodas
- Stopped using disposable items like paper plates and cups, paper towels, and plastic utensils, using instead cloth towels and real plates.
- Used water from the tap instead of buying bottled water
- Cooked from scratch (prepared frozen dinners usually cost more)
- Bought in bulk, but only when they calculated that it was a saving
- Grew a garden
- Looked for clearance items and stocked up when the sale warranted it

- Made a shopping list and stuck to it
- Tried not to waste by using what they bought before it went bad

This may not be the plan that will work for you, but it may stimulate some ideas to create your own. The point is, look for ways that will help you get out of debt. Then make a plan to live within your means. Elder Robert D. Hales put it this way: "To provide providently, we must practice the principles of provident living: joyfully living within our means, being content with what we have, avoiding excessive debt, and diligently saving and preparing for rainy-day emergencies."[14]

Oh, what a concept—"*joyfully* living within our means" and "being *content* with what we have." That is the financial secret to a happy life.

PAY YOUR TITHING

The rest of the secret that makes all of the above work at its best is the law of tithing. The promises associated with paying tithing are legendary. We will not go into much detail about them here, except to highlight a few points on the wisdom of paying tithing as it relates to the wise use of family income.

Elder Robert D. Hales said, "Tithing is the great equitable law, for no matter how rich or poor we are, all of us pay the same one-tenth of our increase annually (see D&C 119:4), and all of us receive blessings so great 'that there shall not be room enough to receive [them]' (Malachi 3:10)."[15]

We cannot resist sharing an experience we had when we were newly married college kids. We were dead broke, almost. We had decided that, no matter what, we would always pay our tithing, and we did. With only a meager income between us—and we mean *meager*— we barely had enough to pay the tithing, rent, and utilities. On this particular day, it would be a week before either of us had a paycheck, of sorts, coming in. We came home for lunch, which would be a can of beans from our pitiful food storage, which consisted of a case of canned beans. That's literally all the food we had in our tiny apartment, and we had no money to buy more.

As we reached the door, to our surprise, we were greeted with a bag of groceries sitting on our doorstep, full of everything we would need for a week other than fresh produce. We had no idea where it came from. That evening the doorbell rang. No one was there; sitting on the doorstep was a gunny sack full of fresh produce, still bearing the bits of dirt as though just plucked from a garden. We knew beyond any doubt that the Lord had blessed us by inspiring some good souls to give us enough food to last the week. No doubt about it, the Lord keeps his promises.

Elder Dallin H. Oaks reminds us of some of those promises:

> In a general conference in 1912, Elder Heber J. Grant declared: "I bear witness—and I know that the witness I bear is true—that the men and the women who have been absolutely honest with God, who have paid their tithing, . . . God has given them wisdom whereby they have been able to utilize the remaining nine-tenths, and it has been of greater value to them, and they have accomplished more with it than they would if they had not been honest with the Lord."[16]

So there you have it—by paying tithing, couples will be given greater wisdom in using the money they have and will accomplish more than if they had used it for something else. We found that to be true as well. When we look back on financially difficult times in our lives, we are amazed that we somehow made it, though we could not imagine how we would at the time.

The Church is full of faithful Saints who can bear witness to these truths. Elder Oaks said, "Some people say, 'I can't afford to pay tithing.' Those who place their faith in the Lord's promises say, 'I can't afford not to pay tithing.'"[17]

SAVINGS AND FOOD STORAGE

We have been counseled to save at least a little every month. No one knows when that extra money may be needed. It's a security blanket for your family. Some may think that's not possible because they can barely pay the bills as is. You may be quite surprised how stashing just $5 a month can add up. Double or triple it when you can, and that security blanket keeps growing. When it's needed for an emergency, use it and start over.

In a national newspaper article titled, "How to Save Money Like a Mormon," the writer said, "Members are encouraged to squirrel away a few months' worth of living expenses."[18] She's right on. In the pamphlet *All Is Safely Gathered In: Family Finances*, the First Presidency wrote, "If you have paid your debts and have a financial reserve . . . , you and your family will feel more secure and enjoy greater peace in your hearts."[19]

In your family plan to save, also include putting away a reserve of food. The plan is to have a food storage that could get you by for at least three months in case of a job loss or other emergency. We are encouraged to do this gradually and not incur any debt in the process. Guidelines are available on lds.org under the heading of Food Storage.

CONCLUSION

As couples wisely use the money with which the Lord has blessed them, they will grow closer to Him and to each other. Jointly they will discover what is important and what isn't.

Elder James E. Faust taught, "It is important to learn to distinguish between wants and needs. It takes self-discipline to avoid the 'buy now, pay later' philosophy and to adopt the 'save now and buy later' practice. . . . Independence means many things. It means . . . being free of personal debt and of the interest and carrying charges required by debt the world over."[20]

Our experience has shown that those who follow this counsel have great peace and love in their marriage. This is the Lord's plan. Satan's is the opposite. His plan is to destroy your marriage, and if he can accomplish that by tempting you to misuse your money, he'll put his whole bag of wiles to work on you. The Savior is more powerful than Satan—by a long shot. There is no way can Satan succeed when we follow the word of the Lord as it comes through our Church leaders.

We conclude with Elder L. Tom Perry's counsel:

> The current cries we hear coming from the great and spacious building tempt us to compete for ownership in the things of this world. . . . Often these items are purchased with borrowed money without giving any thought to providing for our future needs. . . . Wisely we have been counseled to avoid debt as we would

avoid the plague. . . . A well-managed family does not pay interest—it earns it.[21]

Notes

1. "Divorce Study: Financial Arguments Early in Relationships May Predict Divorce," *Huffington Post*, Jul. 16, 2013, http://www.huffingtonpost.com/2013/07/12/divorce-study_n_3587811.html.

2. Gordon B. Hinckley, "To the Boys and to the Men," *Ensign*, Nov. 1998.

3. Ezra Taft Benson, "Prepare Ye," *Ensign*, Jan. 1974.

4. Henry J. Eyring and Robert Eaton, *I Will Lead You Along: The Life of Henry B. Eyring* (Salt Lake City, Utah: Deseret Book, 2013), 253–255.

5. See ibid., 254.

6. Gordon B. Hinckley, "To the Boys and to the Men," *Ensign*, Nov. 1998.

7. "Nearly Broke: Debt Nearly Destroyed Their Marriage," *Marriage Missions International*, http://marriagemissions.com/nearly-broke-debt-nearly-destroyed-their-marriage/.

8. Joseph B. Wirthlin, "Earthly Debts, Heavenly Debts," *Ensign*, May 2004.

9. "Top Five Ways That Money Problems Cause Divorce," *Divorce.com*, http://divorce.com/top-five-ways-money-problems-cause-divorce/.

10. Dallin H. Oaks, "Gambling—Morally Wrong and Politically Unwise," *Ensign*, Jun. 1987.

11. Gordon B. Hinckley, "Gambling," *Ensign*, May 2005.

12. Dieter F. Uchtdorf, "Landing Safely in Turbulence," *Ensign*, Feb. 2016.

13. Crystal Brothers, "Budget Series: Frugal Living (Groceries)," *Serving Joyfully*, May 31, 2012, http://www.servingjoyfully.com/2012/05/31/budget-series-frugal-living-groceries/.

14. Robert D. Hales, "Becoming Provident Providers Temporally and Spiritually," *Ensign*, May 2009.

15. Ibid.

16. Dallin H. Oaks, "Tithing," *Ensign*, May 1994.

17. Ibid.

18. Jennifer Dobner, "Mormons served well by self-reliance in hard times," *Fox News*, Dec. 26, 2008, http://www.foxnews.com/printer_friendly_wires/2008Dec26/0,4675,MormonWelfare,00.html.

19. "Message from the First Presidency," *All Is Safely Gathered In: Family Finances* (The Church of Jesus Christ of Latter-day Saints, 2007).

20. James E. Faust, "The Responsibility for Welfare Rests with Me and My Family," *Ensign*, May 1986.

21. L. Tom Perry, "If Ye Are Prepared Ye Shall Not Fear," *Ensign*, Nov. 1995.

CONCLUSION
Identify and Combat the Enemy

*"Whatsoever is good cometh from God,
and whatsoever is evil cometh from the devil."*
—Alma 5:40

THE FIRST SENTENCE IN *THE Family: A Proclamation to the World,* clearly defines what marriage is and why it is so important: "marriage between a man and a woman is *ordained of God* and . . . the family is *central to the Creator's plan for the eternal destiny of His children"* (emphasis added). Knowing that marriage is ordained of God and is His plan for our eternal destiny puts us on high alert regarding its importance.

In the gospel reference guide, *True to the Faith,* we are told that after a couple makes sacred covenants in the temple, they must "continue in faithfulness in order to receive the blessings of eternal marriage and exaltation."[1] Every husband and wife has the sacred responsibility to do his or her part in safeguarding their marriage.

Elder Robert L. Simpson warned,

> Divorce, with all of its diabolic side effects, threatens the very foundations of society. President Joseph F. Smith observed: "Marriage is the preserver of the human race. Without it, the purposes of God would be frustrated; virtue would be destroyed to give place to vice and corruption, and the earth would be void and empty." Each prophet of this dispensation has said essentially the same thing in his own way.[2]

Understand the Enemy

In order to effectively fight an enemy, we must know who he is and be familiar with his tactics. Otherwise, we have no way of winning the battle. Moroni, the great military captain in the Book of Mormon, showed us countless times how important it was to scope out the plans of the enemy. By learning the strategy of his enemies and continually turning to the Lord for guidance, he was able to come off victorious. This concept works the same for all of us. It's impossible to overcome what we do not know exists. Satan is the enemy, and marriage is one of his prime targets.

In one *Church News* article, members of the Church were given a warning about the reality of Satan: "Warning about the mission of the adversary, the First Presidency of the Church said years ago: 'He is working under such perfect disguise that many do not recognize either him or his methods.'" The article went on to say,

> Just knowing that there is an entity trying to lead the children of God astray is a powerful revelation because not believing an enemy exists puts one at a severe disadvantage. "And behold, others he flattereth away, and telleth them there is no hell; and he saith unto them: I am no devil, for there is none—and thus he whispereth in their ears, until he grasp them with his awful chains, from whence there is no deliverance" (2 Nephi 28:22).[3]

In this book we have revealed some of the methods and strategies Satan uses to destroy marriages in today's world and what we can do to safeguard our families. When we know the plan and methods of the enemy, we have a far greater chance to defeat him and thereby fortify and protect our marriage and children.

Heaven's Protection

"In the parable of the ten virgins, the Lord teaches: 'For they that are wise and have received the truth, and have taken the Holy Spirit for their guide, and have not been deceived—verily I say unto you, they shall not be hewn down and cast into the fire, but shall abide the day' (D&C 45:57)."[4]

Because we may not always be able to recognize some of Satan's methods, once again we are back to knowing that our best weapon for defense in these last days is to take "the Holy Spirit for [our] guide." Elder David A. Bednar said,

> Do we likewise remember to pray earnestly and consistently for that which we should most desire, even the Holy Ghost? Or do we become distracted by the cares of the world and the routine of daily living and take for granted or even neglect this most valuable of all gifts? Receiving the Holy Ghost starts with our sincere and constant desire for His companionship in our lives.[5]

Couples are counseled to pray together every day. We hope that in those prayers husbands and wives are asking the Lord to help them hear the whisperings of the Holy Ghost. We all need His constant companionship. Pray to have it with you always and to be able to discern the warnings the Spirit is giving you.

In a 2015 general conference address, President Thomas S. Monson said,

> [T]he adversary is committed to our failure. He and his hosts are relentless in their efforts to thwart our righteous desires. They represent a grave and constant threat to our eternal salvation unless we are also relentless in our determination and efforts to achieve our goal. The Apostle Peter warns us, "Be vigilant; because your adversary the devil, as a roaring lion, walketh about, seeking whom he may devour" (1 Peter 5:8).[6]

We as Latter-day Saints are blessed with continual reminders of ways we can thwart the adversary and be true to our covenants. By attending our sacrament meetings, Sunday School classes, priesthood, and Relief Society meetings; by listening to leaders at stake conferences and general conferences; and by searching the scriptures and living the teachings therein, we are continually fortified, protected, and prepared for the battle. Add to this regular attendance at the temple, where we are refreshed on the covenants we have made.

These are the blessings from a loving Father in Heaven that help us put on the whole armor of God. These are the things that will safeguard us, our marriage, and our family as we live in the heat of the battle during these last days.

MARRIAGE—OUR PRICELESS GIFT

In a general conference address, Elder F. Burton Howard of the First Quorum of the Seventy said,

> If you want something to last forever, you treat it differently. You shield it and protect it. You never abuse it. You don't expose it to the elements. You don't make it common or ordinary. If it ever becomes tarnished, you lovingly polish it until it gleams like new. It becomes special because you have made it so, and it grows more beautiful and precious as time goes by.
>
> Eternal marriage is just like that. We need to treat it just that way. I pray that we may see it for the priceless gift that it is, in the name of Jesus Christ, amen.[7]

Notes

1. "Marriage," *True to the Faith* (Salt Lake City: The Church of Jesus Christ of Latter-day Saints, 2004), 97–101.

2. Robert L. Simpson, "A Lasting Marriage," *Ensign*, May 1982.

3. "Viewpoint: Be Not Deceived," *Church News*, Mar. 6, 2016, https://www.lds.org/church/news/viewpoint-be-not-deceived?lang=eng.

4. Ibid.

5. David A. Bednar, "Receive the Holy Ghost," *Ensign*, Nov. 2010.

6. Thomas S. Monson, "Keep the Commandments," *Ensign*, Nov. 2015.

7. F. Burton Howard, "Eternal Marriage," *Ensign*, May 2003.

ABOUT THE AUTHORS

GARY LUNDBERG IS A LICENSED marriage and family therapist, speaker, and singer, and is a clinical member of the American Association for Marriage and Family Therapy. Born and raised in Washington, DC, he served seven years as a fighter pilot in the US Air Force.

Joy Lundberg is a writer, lyricist, and has written over 200 published songs with composer Janice Kapp Perry. She served seven years as a script writer for the Tabernacle Choir broadcast *Music and the Spoken Word* and six years on the Church Curriculum Committee. She was raised on a farm in Vale, Oregon.

Gary and Joy are the authors of the popular book on relationships *I Don't Have to Make Everything All Better*, published by Penguin Group. They are the authors of *Love That Lasts: 14 secrets to a more joyful, passionate, and fulfilling marriage*, published by Covenant Communications. They also self-published the novel on improving in-law relationships, *Meeting Amazing Grace*, and a book to help youth protect their sexual purity, titled *On Guard*.

Besides writing and speaking together for many years, their relationship has been enriched and stretched by church callings, mission service, temple service, and most of all by being parents of five terrific and diverse children. They are filled with gratitude to these children for giving them twenty amazing grandchildren. Gary and Joy live in Provo, Utah. Their website is garyjoylundberg.com.